MACHINE AND POWER TOOLS FOR WOODWORK

MACHINE AND POWER TOOLS FOR WOODWORK

Gordon Stokes

BELL & HYMAN

First published 1986 by
Bell & Hyman Limited
Denmark House
37–39 Queen Elizabeth Street
London SE1 2QB

Designed by Paul Turner, Stonecastle
Graphics
Drawings by Arthur Dalton
Typeset by August Filmsetting, Haydock,
St. Helens
Printed in Great Britain by BAS Printers Limited,
Over Wallop, Hampshire

**British Library in Cataloguing Publication
Data**

Stokes, Gordon
 Machine and power tools for Woodwork
  1. Machine-tools
  I. Title
  621–9′02   TJ1185

ISBN 0–7135–2609–2

Acknowledgements

The author and publishers would like to thank
the following manufacturers for photographs
and machines featured in photographs and
line drawings: Avon; Black and Decker;
Bosch; De Walt; Elu; Luna Tools; Hegner;
Startrite; Wolf.

Cover photographs courtesy of Black and
Decker, De Walt, Elu and Hegner.

CONTENTS

1 Introduction 7

2 Safety 9

3 Drills and Drilling Techniques 12
    Hand Held Drills 12
    Bench Drills 14

4 The Circular Saw 21
    Using the Sawbench 28
    Portable Circular Saws 38

5 The Radial Arm Saw 44

6 Bandsaws 55

7 Jigsaws 66

8 Planers 70
    Surface Planers 70
    Planer Thicknessers 75
    Portable Planers 80

9 Mortisers 82

10 The Portable Router 87

11 Sanders 95
    Belt Sanders 95
    Orbital Sanders 98
    Disc Sanders 100
    Sanding Attachments 101

12 Lathes 105
    Copying Attachments 112

13 The Grinder 114

14 Universals 117
    The Spindle Moulder 118

15 The Powered Fretsaw 123

16 The Flat Dowel Jointer 128

17 Miscellaneous Power Tools 131
    The Electric Screwdriver 132
    Blowers 133

18 Woodworking Joints 135

Glossary 141

Index 142

1
INTRODUCTION

This book aims to give a broad view of the types of machine currently available for home workshop and small business use, and to indicate how the capabilities of these machines can be exploited efficiently and safely. Any book which attempted to cover all aspects and applications of every tool would have to run into two or three volumes, and indeed some power tools, for example routers and radial arm saws, have been the subject of complete books. So the descriptions here are necessarily brief.

It is hoped, however, that a thorough study of this volume will enable the reader to overcome the common problem of being unable to see the wood for the trees when browsing in a tool store or at a woodworking exhibition. The precise requirements of an individual when setting up a power tool workshop will vary according to the type of woodwork envisaged, and it is a great help to have some ideas of the merits and demerits of specific machines. Safety is naturally of paramount importance, and considerable emphasis has been given to it here. Not all potential dangers in power tool woodwork are obvious, but most become so once they have been pointed out. Accidents do happen in machine woodworking, but almost invariably they could have been avoided by some preliminary study of safety aspects.

The quality of machines varies widely, some being excellent, while others which perhaps appear attractive in terms of initial capital outlay may well be poorly designed and constructed, and so at best inaccurate, and at worst dangerous. It is invariably better to wait until sufficient funds are available for the purchase of

a good quality machine, than to buy a cheap and cheerful one.

Quite apart from being unable to judge the quality and potential accuracy of a specific machine, the novice often has extreme difficulty in obtaining truly unbiased advice from someone who has a wide experience of using or testing different makes and models. The chap up the road who has a machine or two may swear by a certain make which he happens to own, rather than admit that he made a mistake when he bought it. On the other hand he may swear about it rather than by it, though this could be because he has never learned to use it properly, or to set it up correctly. How is the beginner to know whether he is a very knowledgeable and skilled man doing his best to give sound advice? Having demonstrated machinery of one sort or another at the major woodworking shows for around twenty years, both here and overseas, I have had many hundreds of conversations with people who were quite obviously lost in a mass of conflicting advice obtained from a large number of sources. This, of course, is an extremely frustrating situation, which will be familiar to many who have been involved in their first purchase of home computers, hi-fi equipment, cameras, or whatever.

It might seem that the sensible approach is to seek advice from a tool store, or at a woodworking show. In the latter case there will almost certainly be an opportunity to see the machines in action, but it is as well to remember that the operators are skilled demonstrators and trained salesmen, who make it all look very simple. They are also paid to promote the sale of the range of machines on their stand, not those on the neighbouring ones. It is highly probable that the timber used for the demonstration will be softwood of some kind, and it is wise to insist upon seeing a machine perform on some hardwood such as beech or oak. This request may not be greeted with enthusiasm, and is likely to be met with the standard reply, which is that none is available because it is too expensive to use for demonstrations. Few timbers are too expensive to be used in situations where two or three cuts may clinch the sale of an expensive machine, and if you really want to get at the truth, why not take some hardwood with you, preferably a bit with some awkward grain in it! A demonstrator who has a good machine will accept the challenge, and if the tool does a good job you are beginning to get somewhere.

Magazines do try to be impartial, but their life blood is the advertising matter they contain. Good manufacturers do not object to constructive criticism, however, although the bad ones squeal loudly, and to be fair there is often objective criticism and sound advice in the leading woodworking publications. When criticism is made it is interesting to note that standard replies are quickly produced for use when potential customers mention the specific point. One of the best I have heard – and there have been many – concerned a certain make of bandsaw, no longer extant, which had not succeeded in being totally useless, but deserved an A for effort in its attempt to be so. It made an unbelievable noise when running ('That's the extra powerful motor, sir') and the blade moved backwards and forwards over a good quarter of an inch when in motion. One retailer who had unwisely involved himself in the sale of these things not only had an answer, but managed to turn an extremely bad fault into a virtue. ('That's to give the blade a chance to clear the dust, sir'). When the bandsaw chapter in this book has been studied, the humour of this will be apparent. Although my Latin is now rusty, 'caveat emptor' has remained firmly in my head: Let the buyer beware!

Please don't think after all this that everyone is out to cheat you. That is simply not so, and the majority of people make a genuine effort to advise their customers truthfully. The point is that one may just be talking to one of the few who do not. The most likely source of impartial advice based upon empirical knowledge is among the well-known woodworking writers, who cannot afford to be other than impartial, because they have to preserve their credibility, and it is a serious mistake for an author or journalist in this field to become directly affiliated with any manufacturer.

Perhaps more important, and not sufficiently realised, is the fact that most of us are quite willing to have a quick chat on the telephone (no letters, please, they take time to answer) with anyone who is about to spend quite a lot of money, and is worried about choice of machine. My number is in the book, which I hope you will enjoy. It should provide a few signposts to help you through the minefield.

Please note that guards must be used at all times when machining timber, and that any photograph or drawing in this book which does not show a guard is so presented for the sake of clarity.

GORDON STOKES
BATH
1986.

2
SAFETY

The vast majority of workshop hazards can be classified as electrical, tooling, or material: electric shock; damage to the person caused by blades, knives, moulding cutters, or other forms of tooling; or caused by material being ejected at speed and under power from a machine. It is necessary to draw a line at some point, however, so I have not included such things as purple thumbs derived from inaccurate hammer blows or damaged groins which result from walking into mortiser handles. The subconscious masochist will always find fulfilment.

Electrical Hazards

Cables fitted to machines must always be of the correct specification, and if there is any doubt as to their condition after long use they must be replaced. They do not enjoy constantly being walked on, which will eventually damage the internal insulation, and may cause a fire, so if they must be routed from a wall to a centrally placed machine they should be taken overhead. Cables trailing on the floor can also trip someone, who may fall towards a set of rotating cutters. Regular checks should be made to establish that the connections to both plug and machine are in good order, and if a fuse fails in the plug or the machine it must never be replaced by one of a higher rating.

There are also mice, which love bright orange nests made from sander dust extraction bags, and also have an engaging habit of chewing insulation. My workshop is an old chapel, and is periodically used as a hostel by the odd rodent or two. I therefore always switch all power off at the meter inside the door when I leave, so that if they should chew off enough insulation to start a fire I will at least be there when it happens.

It can be unwise to assume that a new machine, which has recently been delivered, will be correctly wired, so it is always as well to have a look at the connections, or ask a knowledgeable friend to do so. Those with little or no knowledge of electricity should not be ashamed to call in an electrician, since mistakes can be lethal.

Tooling Hazards

Injuries from tooling do occur, and are sometimes severe, but they are often the result of carelessness or over confidence, and they can be avoided. Workshop floors can cause accidents which may well involve workers falling against moving machines either because they have been allowed to become littered with small offcuts, or due to the fact that wooden floors can be very slippery when covered in sawdust. In this respect rubber soled shoes are preferable.

When operating machinery it is dangerous to wear a tie, and sleeves should always be rolled securely back out of the way. In addition to this, loose clothing which can flap about is a distinct hazard, and must be avoided.

It is unfortunate that beginners are sometimes involved in accidents or frightening incidents because they are apprehensive, and not sufficiently positive in what they do. The same syndrome is evident among inexperienced drivers, but it is difficult to act positively and with confidence in the early stages. The problem is greatly reduced, however, in cases where the operator knows the hazards, and so does not have to learn about them the hard way. Demonstrators at woodworking shows normally take heavy cuts with machines to show their full capabilities, but heavy cutting of this kind is dangerous for beginners, and where a large amount of wood is to be removed with a spindle moulder for example, it is sensible to take off a reasonable amount with one cut, then reset the tool and complete the job. It may even be quicker in the long run, because heavy cuts may tear the wood, and not produce the best surface finishes. It may be quicker to make one cut than to make two, but the abrasive work required to clean a torn surface can be extensive and time consuming.

Maintenance

All machinery requires some maintenance, which usually requires little time, but it should be carried out regularly, in accordance with the manufacturer's instructions. When cutters are becoming dull they should be sharpened, since just as blunt hand tools cause accidents by behaving unpredictably, blunt machine blades or cutters may suddenly reject a workpiece. Signs of dull edges are the need for heavy pressure to feed the work, and excessive noise or scorch marks on machined timber. Wood is difficult to hold down over blunt planer knives, and may rise from the table and attempt to 'climb' a dull circular sawblade. The rule is 'if in doubt, sharpen'.

Guards

Guards are vital, but only effective if well designed, and always positioned so that when the machine is in use it is not possible for a hand to contact blade or cutter. Many machines are belt driven, and the belts must always be fully guarded or an accident will eventually occur. The method of feeding material is also very important, in that the work is always fed into the rotation of the cutter rather than with it, which will be clear from the various illustrations. There is one exception, in the case of cross-cutting with a radial arm saw, but here it is the blade which travels, not the wood.

Push Sticks

Push sticks or pusher blocks should be within reach when a cut is started, or there will be a temptation to finish the cut without one, so perhaps placing the hands at risk. Never flick off-cuts from machine tables, however alluring the idea may be, it is safer to push them away with a piece of wood, or to leave them until the machine has stopped. When large workpieces are machined it is important to check that the cut can be completed without the wood meeting any obstruction, which is often not the case in small workshops. Sheet material should be cut to approximate size with a handsaw or a jigsaw, so that manageable pieces can be taken to the machine for final cutting to accurate dimensions. If sheet material has an appreciable projection over the side of a sawbench, some form of support should be provided, or the operation will be potentially dangerous.

Obstructions

Small tools must not be left on machine tables, and a check should always be made after any adjustments to confirm that there is no obstruction to free rotation of blade or cutters. Never leave machines running when they are not in use, and note that really sensible workers take the plug from the socket. Visitors to workshops have a habit of twiddling knobs!

If a dust extraction unit is available, it should be used as much as possible, both to keep the atmosphere suitable for breathing purposes, and to avoid the nasty accidents which sometimes occur when an operator succumbs to the temptation to remove unwanted shavings from a machine table by hand. This sort of thing is highly dangerous, and must never be attempted until the tool has been switched off, and has come to rest.

All workpieces should be carefully checked for splits or other faults which might cause them to shatter while being machined.

Operator Hazards

The safety of all power tools depends on the care and concentration of the person using them. Many people regard motor cycles as dangerous, but these machines do not normally have accidents in showrooms. They are certainly dangerous in untrained hands, as are woodworking machines, but one must remember that circular saws do not usually have the ability to injure people who keep their bodies well clear of the blade. My point here is that one of the great steps towards safety with equipment of this nature is to accept that we are all fallible, and that the potential dangers of machine woodworking, motorcycling, or any other hazardous pursuit lie almost entirely in the actions of the operator, and rarely in the machine.

Using machinery when feeling unwell or very tired is not a good idea, since it is then easy to be careless. Beware also of those days when irritability is evident, or there is felt to be a need to hurry the job. Occasions like this are dangerous.

Finally, concentrate at all times, and if you must buy a spindle moulder, do take a good practical course before using it.

3
DRILLS AND DRILLING TECHNIQUES

Electrically driven drills of one sort or another are used in home woodwork workshops for a variety of purposes, quite apart from the obvious need to drill holes. Most people are now very familiar with the hand held drill, which is really little more than a motor in a suitably shaped case, equipped with a chuck which enables it to grip drills, bits, small sanders, and the like. This is a useful tool for general work, but when the need arises for the accurate and precise drilling of holes at exact and specific angles relative to the work surface, some form of bench or pillar drill is called for. It is also necessary at times to bore large holes, perhaps two or three inches in diameter, which cannot be done with the hand held drill. Many workers, in fact, would rate a bench or floor standing 'drill press' high on their list of priorities when equipping a workshop.

Amateur woodworkers are by nature ingenious and inventive, and drills, whether bench mounted or hand held, are excellent sources of power, and capable of much more than the simple drilling of holes. In the case of hand drills, however, some thought should be given to selection of type before purchase, otherwise money may be wasted. Those who require a hand held drill for general work around the home will usually find a consumer drill, designed for occasional home use, to be quite satisfactory. This is the least expensive type, but if used for the occasional drilling of holes, as for example in putting up the odd shelf, and perhaps a little light sanding work with a drum or small disc sander, it can provide years of service. The chuck size is significant, since it indicates the maximum diameter of cutter shank which can be used.

HAND HELD DRILLS

Chuck Sizes

The chuck sizes which concern the home worker are quarter, three eighths, and half inch, and the power of the drill will vary accordingly. The main enemy of hand held drills is overloading, which will cause overheating, and thus early failure of the motor. The larger the chuck size, the greater the power, and of course the price. Consumer drills are fine for occasional light use, but should be used intermittently and given frequent opportunities to cool down. Where long periods of hard work are envisaged, however, they are unsuitable, and a drill of the professional or industrial variety should be selected. These are considerably more expensive, but are designed to stand up to regular daily use for long periods.

Speed

For light woodworking operations a single speed drill will suffice, but some versions offer several speeds, selectable by means of a dial or by varying the trigger pressure. Some drills have 'infinitely variable' speed controls, which are operated electronically rather than by trains of gears, and in some applications these can be useful.

Safety

Perhaps because drills seem fairly harmless devices by comparison with circular saws and planers, they are sometimes treated in a rather cavalier manner by their users, but safety precautions must be observed with all power tools if injuries are to be avoided. Having said that, I will admit to having injured my own hand on one occasion when changing a drill bit. I had switched the tool off at the wall socket, or so I believed, but in fact I had operated the wrong switch of a pair, and there is no excuse for this kind of thing. The plug must ALWAYS be removed from the socket.

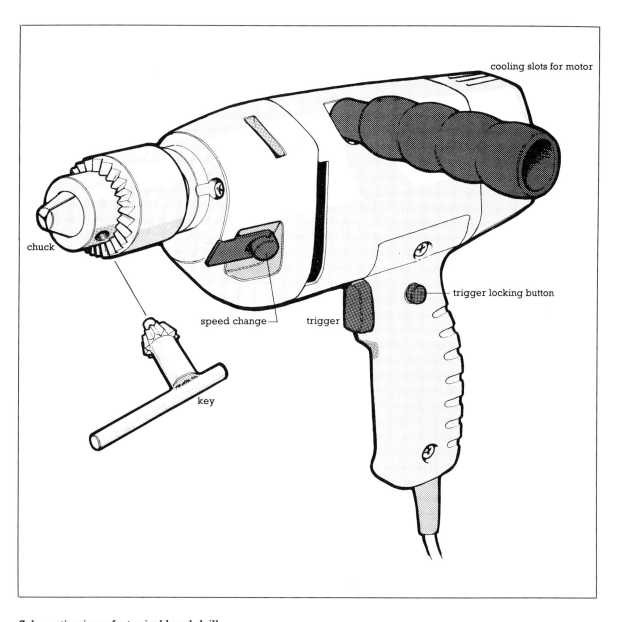

Schematic view of a typical hand drill.

Attachments

Hand held electric drills passed through quite a long period in which they were used as power sources to drive a wide variety of attachments, such as jigsaws, circular saws, sanders, planing devices, and the like. The problems with this were mainly that changing over from one attachment to another was frequently a slow and irritating procedure, and that some attachments were apt to overload the drill, especially on heavy cuts with blunt blades, so they are declining in popularity. Attachments are still available for hand drills, but the self powered hand tool is now far more popular, and can be quite effective for some operations.

Drill Stands

Most manufacturers offer as an accessory some form of drill stand, into which the drill can be fitted. This gives a small version of the bench drill, and for the hobbyist it offers some versatility, in that the drill can be removed from the stand when required for freehand work. The quality of such drill stands does vary, and some are very poorly designed. The heavier the construction the better, and if possible it is as well to try one in a store before buying. Check to see that the drill can be fitted and removed quickly and easily, and that the operating lever and drill carriage move smoothly.

BENCH DRILLS

A portable hand held electric drill is almost essential equipment in the workshop, but there is nothing like a bench or pillar drill for serious work. This machine is known in America as a drill press, and is available either as a bench mounted tool, or as a free-standing item of equipment, offering considerable power and frequently a wide range of speeds. The power source is usually an induction motor of three quarter or one horsepower, but half horsepower units may be found on some models. A good quality motor is essential, since large hole drilling in hardwoods or metal requires considerable power. The number of selectable speeds varies among models, some offering as many as twelve.

Construction

Designs do vary slightly, but in general terms the machine consists of a heavy steel base, or bottom table, at the rear of which a stout cylindrical steel column is mounted vertically. The drilling head with motor and speed change system is fixed to the top of the column, and a second table is fitted to the column between the base and the drilling head. This is the main table, and can be slid up or down the column, and clamped in any desired position. It is usual, and desirable, for this table to be provided with tilting facilities and a clamping mechanism, so

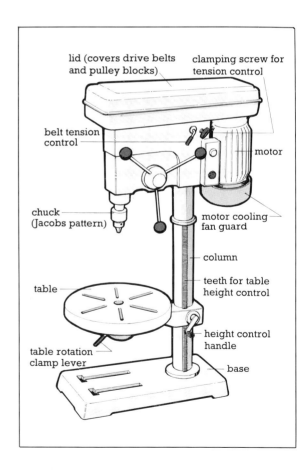

A typical heavy duty bench drill.

that it can be set with its surface at angles other than ninety degrees to the horizontal.

On some machines the main table is moved manually up or down the column, but it is worth spending a little more money to obtain a mechanical rise and fall system, as on the machine shown here. This makes adjustments quick and simple, but it must be so designed as not to interfere with the facility of rotating the table around the column. This is important, since when drilling is done into the end of a long workpiece, the main table is swung out of the way, and the bottom table is used.

Pulley drive system on twelve speed drill. Belt tensioning lever (bottom centre) moves motor to slacken or tighten belt. Turnscrews, one at right of lever, one on other side of drill, lock tool at a given setting.

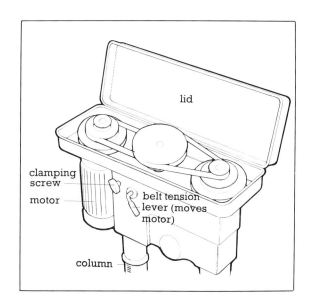

Construction of the bench drill. Belts should not be adjusted tightly.

Startrite floor standing pillar drill, very useful for long workpieces.

The motor is mounted vertically at the rear of the drilling head, and drives a vertical spindle, mounted at the front, to which is attached a drill chuck. Speed settings are made through a system of stepped pulleys, and the motor can be moved towards or away from the operator to slacken or tighten the drive belt, and to provide a means of freeing it for speed changing. The spindle has a quill feed, which allows it to be brought downward when drilling, and it is returned to its original position by spring pressure when the operating lever is released. Most machines have a control which can be set for predetermined depth, which is very useful, and some also have a scale from which the depth of penetration of the drill bit can be read.

Chucks

The chuck which is fitted to bench drills is a heavy duty Jacobs pattern, and must be of high quality. It is also extremely important for this chuck to run true, without any wobble. This can be checked in the showroom before purchase if a thin steel rod such as a tommy bar is clamped in the chuck, and the latter is then rotated by pulling on the drive belt. If the end of the rod shows any tendency to wobble, the sensible move is to find another machine which will pass the test. The chuck on a bench drill is opened and closed by means of a chuck key such as is used on the normal hand held electric drill, and it is important to form the habit of removing this key from the chuck as soon as an adjustment has been made, since it can be ejected with some force when the machine is started, and could cause an injury.

Noise

A point well worth noting is that good bench drills run extremely quietly, and bad ones are often quite noisy, so it is advisable to ask to hear the machine run before parting with any cash. It is a simple enough matter to slip a plug on and run the tool, so if the vendor is reluctant it may pay to look elsewhere. In connection with noise, it should be noted that these machines do not need heavy belt tension, in fact this is not good for any machine. If too much tension is applied to the drive belt the noise level will be unacceptable, but a slight adjustment of the motor position will put this right.

Uses of Bench Drills

Bench drills can of course be used for drilling

materials other than wood, and some users will have frequent requirements for holes in metal, or various kinds of plastic sheet. Small workpieces, particularly of metal, should be firmly clamped, or the cutter may grab and spin them violently, causing hand injuries. This can apply with wood, which is dangerous and undesirable, but a hand held piece of metal could cause a very serious injury in such circumstances, so it is never worth taking chances.

Tables

The clamping of workpieces for drilling is by no means difficult, but it must be done carefully, so that there is no chance of a clamp slipping suddenly. The tables of bench drills are slotted to permit the passage of bolts, so that wooden sub tables, constructed in the workshop, can be fitted. These can be modified in many ways to form jigs for repetition work, to facilitate angled drilling, and so on. Sub tables are usually constructed from chipboard, blockboard, or thick plywood, and are worth taking some time over, as they may be in use for many years. One of the simplest and most effective forms of sub table is a flat board bolted to the main table, with the bolt heads sunk below the surface of the wood.

The drill table must be of solid construction, as here. This one is capable of being tilted, rotated, or swung out of the way for the drilling of extra long workpieces, which rest on the drill base.

16

A wooden fence is fitted to this on edge, at ninety degrees, and workpieces can be firmly held in position against it by means of good quality clamps. If the bolts holding the sub table to the main table pass through slots, and are fitted with wing nuts, the fence can be adjusted in relation to the drill bit.

A hole is always provided at the centre of the table, to allow a drill bit to emerge from the work without obstruction, but when wood is being drilled some scrap timber should always be placed between work and table, or there will be spelching as the cutter breaks through and knocks the fibres of the timbers outwards, producing a ragged effect.

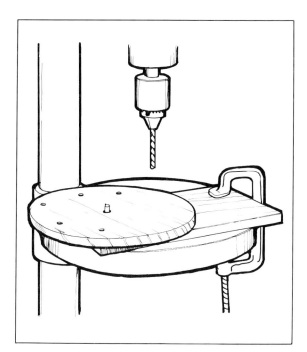

Jig for drilling holes equidistant from the centre of a disc. Note the scrap wood under the workpiece to protect the table.

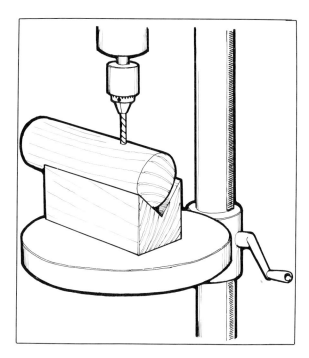

Radial drilling into turned work is simplified by making a 'V' block and centring the drill to the bottom of the 'V'.

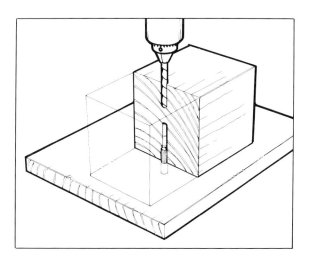

If the faces of the workpiece are parallel to each other, a hole can be drilled through the job even with a short drill. The locating pin in the supporting wood ensures alignment.

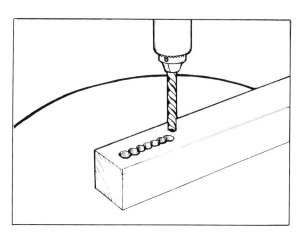

Mortises can be produced by drilling out most of the waste, then cleaning up with a sharp chisel.

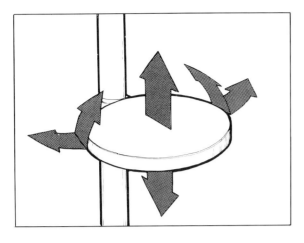

The drilling table can be swung round the pillar, moved up and down, and tilted.

(a) Single twist or hollow spiral bit. (b) Double spur bit. (c) Alternative double spur (solid centre bit). (d) Saw toothed bit. (e) Short spur bit. (f) Spade or flat bit. (g) Special countersink or river's bit.

Drill Bits and Cutters

There are many types of drill bit and cutter, most of which can be used on wood, but there is some element of confusion in view of the fact that the names used for different examples tend to vary from one part of the country to another. A number of the more popular varieties can be seen in the illustrations, with indications as to purpose. When drilling in wood, excess pressure should be avoided, the cutter being allowed to make its way through the timber without force, and it will often help to lift the drill from the work occasionally to assist chip clearance. If the cutter cannot clear its chips properly it will overheat and the temper of the steel will be drawn.

In general it is safe to say that large cutters require low speeds, and smaller ones need high speeds, but there are exceptions. One example is the flat or spade bit, which in fact has a scraping action, and requires a high speed even when its larger sizes are used. Saw toothed bits and Forstner bits, on the other hand, are very expensive, especially in the large sizes, and should rotate at a very low speed or they will soon be ruined.

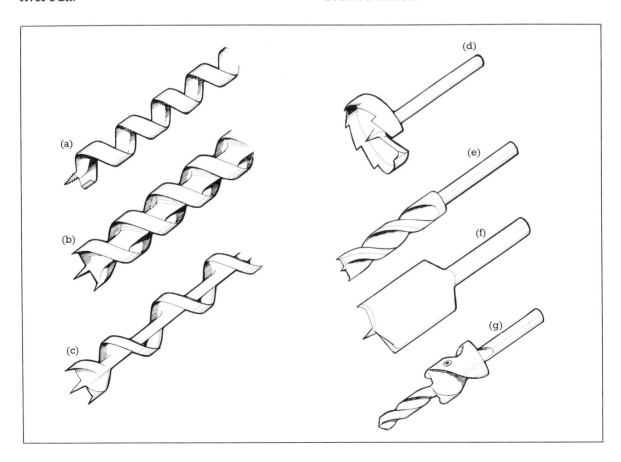

Clamps

Timber is frequently held by clamps when being processed by machinery, and it is a big mistake to use cheap and inefficient clamps. I have now been using the type shown in the various photographs for many years, without trouble, and although they are not the cheapest available they are certainly worth their price. They are known as Jet Clamps, designed and manufactured by TMT Design Ltd., of Leamington Spa, and they form part of an excellent clamping system which is well worth investigating. There is insufficient space available here for a full description of what can be done with these devices, but I do consider the use of good clamps to be a safety factor, and I am sure that the makers would provide full details if requested.

Sanding Attachments

The use of small drum or bobbin sanders on bench drills is quite common, and can be very effective for cleaning up edges, but it is worth making a special sub table for the purpose. This will have a hole drilled at its centre, a little larger than the sander diameter, so that the sander can run with its lower edge just below the surface of the table. This enables all the edges of the wood to be sanded, and the movement of the timber should be against the rotation of the sander. Too much pressure and/or too slow a feed rate will create excessive heat, and scorch the wood. Work of this kind definitely calls for a dust extractor, or a good sanding mask, especially if there is much of it to be done. The best speed for the machine in this work will depend upon the diameter of the sander, and can quickly be established by a few trial runs.

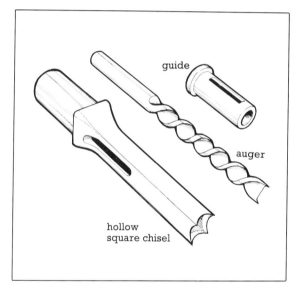

A chisel, auger, and guide, as used for mortising with the bench drill.

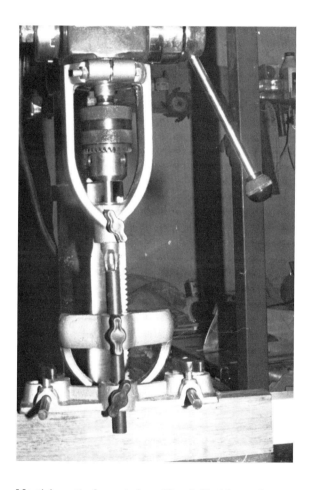

Mortising attachments for pillar drills (shown in reverse to show clamping system) use hollow square chisels and augers. This is the best approach for the average home woodworker, who cuts mortises only occasionally.

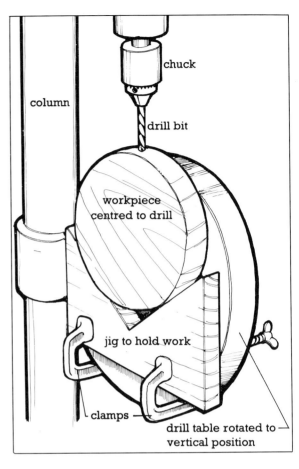

Pillar drill fitted with large Forstner bit. Note use of scrap wood under workpiece, to protect cutter and table, and to reduce spelching as cutter breaks through.

The user of a bench drill soon becomes able to devise ways to hold awkward workpieces.

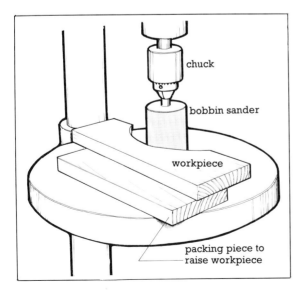

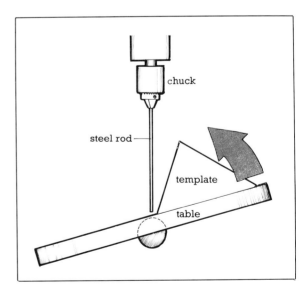

Bobbin sanding on a pillar drill.

Accurate angle setting on drill table, using a template.

4

THE CIRCULAR SAW

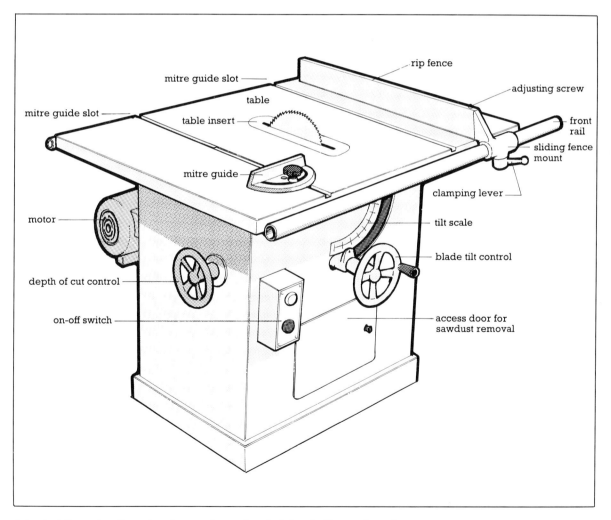

A typical floor standing circular saw (guard and riving knife not shown).

For most woodworkers the first step on the road to workshop mechanisation is the purchase of a circular saw, which if well designed and constructed, and sensibly used, will be a very worthwhile investment. In view of the wide variety of bench or floor mounted machinery which comes into this category, however, some research is essential if expensive mistakes are to be avoided. The aims will normally be to install a machine which will remove the drudgery from the processes of cutting timber to required length and width, and provide a high degree of accuracy. Circular saws are capable of a great deal more than this, but the prime prerequisites, as with all machinery, are safety and efficiency, in that order.

Anyone considering the purchase of a tool of this kind for the first time is likely to find that browsing in tool stores or at the big shows merely serves to confuse, and there is always the danger of being talked into the purchase of a machine which is in some respects unsuitable for the specific requirements of the individual. Certain facilities which are incorporated on expensive saws may appear to be very interesting and desirable, but they may not be worthwhile if they increase the price of the tool considerably, but are rarely used, and there may be other ways of approaching the problems which they are intended to solve.

My intention here is to give guidance on the selection and safe use of these saws and sawbenches, concentrating on their more usual functions. Circular saws of any kind can be dangerous in the hands of careless people, but they can also be good servants if they are understood and treated with respect. These tools do not make unprovoked attacks upon their users, and if the hands are kept well clear of the blade at all times, it follows that they will never contact it. If the safety points contained in this book are borne in mind, and faithfully adhered to, great benefit and enjoyment can be derived from such equipment.

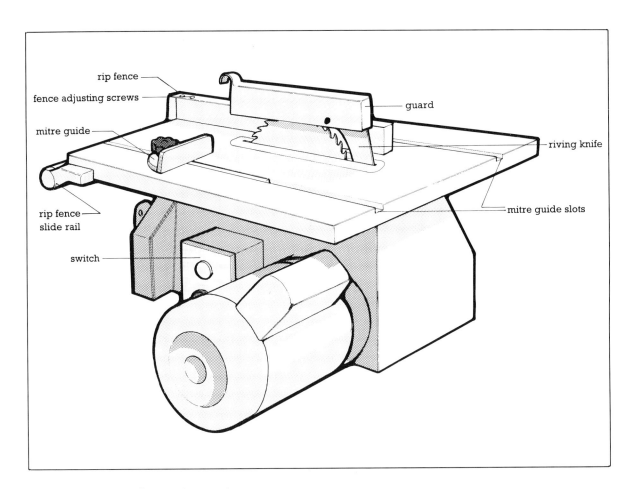

A small circular saw for bench mounting.

Construction

In basic terms a circular saw consists of a motor driven spindle or shaft mounted in a box or frame, the shaft carrying a circular steel blade which has teeth cut around its periphery. The blade can be set to project through the flat upper surface (table) of the machine, this projection being capable of adjustment by the operator. This is achieved on some machines by moving the spindle, and with it the blade. On cheaper machines the table itself is moved up or down relative to the blade. In addition to this, there may be provision for altering the angle between the surfaces of blade and table, permitting angled cuts to be made.

In this respect there is a major difference between expensive machines and cheaper versions, in that in the former case the blade can be tilted relative to the table, whereas on cheaper sawbenches the table is tilted and the blade remains vertical. Machines on which the blade is tilted are known as tilting arbor saws, and they are expensive because of the complexity of the tilting mechanism. Movement of table or blade in the vertical plane is referred to as 'rise and fall'. It will be clear, therefore, that on tilting arbor saws the table remains horizontal in all operations, and at a constant height, but cheaper machines, on which the table is moved, do perform quite adequately.

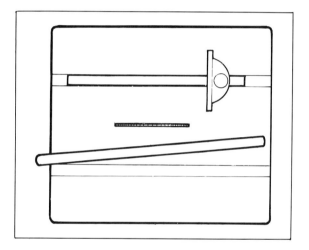

Using the circular saw (in all these diagrams and those on p. 24 the timber is fed from left to right).

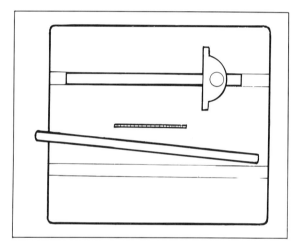

Left and above: rip fence is not aligned with blade.

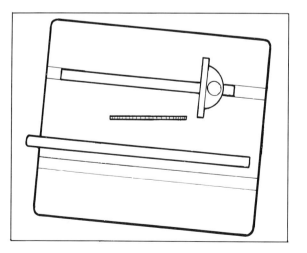

Above: rip fence and mitre guide are set correctly to the table but the table is out of alignment with the

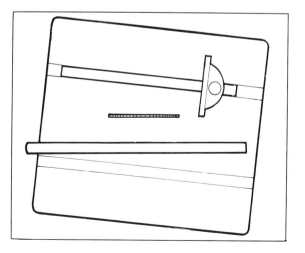

blade. If this error is corrected by moving the rip fence the mitre guide remains incorrect (right).

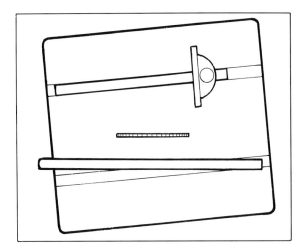

The table is not aligned with the blade.

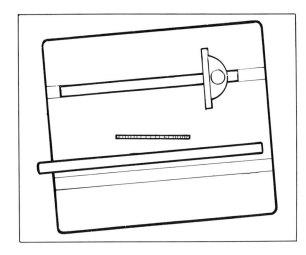

Neither the rip fence nor the guide would operate correctly in this condition, but both would be correctly set if the table was adjusted true to the blade.

Selecting a Sawbench

In order to make a satisfactory choice from the large number of differing types offered in tool shops and magazine advertisements, the intending purchaser requires an understanding of the circular saw in its basic form, and an appreciation of the values of the various features with which these machines can be provided. A sawbench should be selected firstly on the quality of design and construction, which can go a long way towards providing safety and accuracy. The second factor to be considered is the type of work for which the tool is intended. The various components and capacities of sawbenches are discussed in the following section, to assist those who may be contemplating the installation of a floor or bench mounted model.

Sawbenches, unlike radial arm saws, require a fair amount of space all round, and so cannot be situated against a wall. Some workpieces will be quite long, and there must be room for these to pass to the rear of the machine when being ripped, and to project on either side when being crosscut. There must also be space in front of the sawbench for long sections of wood at the start of a ripping cut, and for the operator to work in comfort and safety. These machines therefore tend to occupy a central position in the workshop.

Motors

When intended for home or small business use, sawbenches normally provide a maximum depth of cut which may be as low as two inches or as high as four, but it is worth noting that maximum depth cutting, especially in hardwoods, calls for a fair amount of power, particularly when ripping. The better machines have motor overload protection, in the form of thermal switches, which cause the motor to cut out when it reaches a certain temperature. The machine cannot be restarted after this switch has operated, until a reset button has been pressed, but it is not possible to use this button until the motor has cooled sufficiently.

Motors used in woodworking environments should be of the totally enclosed variety, since a considerable amount of dust is produced in some operations. A draught of air is required around the motor casing for cooling purposes, this being provided by a fan mounted at one end, and covered by a plastic cowl. The fan draws air in, and forces it out around the casing, which often has ribs to provide a greater surface area and so assist the cooling process. The speed of the motor will not normally concern the woodworker, since it is related to blade diameter to provide efficient cutting together with satisfactory blade life, and this relationship will have been dealt with by the makers.

Motors supplied with good quality machines can safely be assumed to have sufficient power for their intended purpose, and this will vary according to blade diameter. As a guide, sawbenches with eight inch diameter blades are normally fitted with motors of half horsepower capacity, ten inch machines will have three quarter or one horsepower, and those with twelve inch blades may be fitted with one and a half or two horsepower motors.

Controls

The raising, lowering, or tilting of blade or table is normally achieved by means of hand-wheels, some form of locking device being provided to secure the machine at a given setting. The movement of these controls should be smooth and free, or they will be a source of continual irritation, and possibly of inaccuracy.

The Saw Table

Given adequate power, suitable speed, and a sharp blade of good quality, the performance of a sawbench will depend to a great extent upon the quality of the table itself, and upon its associated accessories, the rip fence and the mitre guide.

Where a high degree of precision is required, as in cabinet making, the saw table should be of cast steel which has been machined to fine limits, so producing a completely flat surface which will remain flat throughout the life of the machine. Such tables are expensive, but well worth their cost. Alternatives are cast alloy or pressed sheet steel. Both are in common use on lighter machines, and if well made will give reasonable results.

Table Inserts

The better machines are fitted with table inserts, which can be removed when the need arises to use a dado head or a moulding block in place of the sawblade. These may be made of steel, alloy, plastic, or wood, and it is a good idea when selecting a sawbench to check that the blade (or the table) can be tilted without the teeth of the saw contacting the insert. If this is not so, the insert may have to be removed for some angle cutting, which is undesirable. The purpose of the table insert is to provide support for the wood close up to the blade, and to prevent small pieces from being dragged down.

Mitre Guides

Reference to the illustrations will clarify these points, and it will be noted that ideally the table should have two grooves or slots, one each side of the blade, into which the runner of a mitre guide can be fitted. Some machines have only one such slot, and many cheap sawbenches have none.

Given a mitre guide of good quality, with a runner which fits the table slot correctly, precision crosscutting is possible. A mitre guide is a metal fence, attached to a table runner, and fitted with a protractor scale. A locking screw is provided to enable the fence to be secured at a desired setting. Adjustment is made by slack-

A Startrite sawbench fitted with support tables for large panels. Note adjustable fence on right hand table. Left hand table slides with panel held square to blade by guide fence. Large panels can be handled easily and safely by one person.

ening the retaining screw, pivoting the fence as required, then tightening securely. Cutting operations consist of fitting the runner into the table slot, placing the workpiece firmly against the mitre fence, and moving guide and wood forward until the cut is completed.

In the case of a new machine, the guide should always be checked with the aid of a woodworker's square, to ensure that when the angle between the fence and the blade is ninety degrees, the pointer on the mitre guide scale is at zero. If this is not so, the pointer must be adjusted to read zero, and firmly locked in place. Angles other than ninety degrees can then be set quite accurately from the scale.

Many mitre guides have holes in the vertical part of the fence, through which screws can be passed to attach home made wooden sub-fences, the purposes of which will be dealt with later. Note that it is better for the runner to be slightly tight in the table grooves than a slack fit, in the interests of accuracy, and a piece of beeswax or a stub of candle rubbed in the groove will ensure free movement.

Rip Fences

Rip fences are used when timber is sawn along its length, and are a very important feature of sawbenches. They must at all times be parallel to the table grooves, and the sawtable must be parallel to both grooves and rip fence. It is unfortunate that many cheap sawbenches do not allow fine adjustment of some of these essential features, and new owners may not discover this until the machine has been in use for a while, so when purchasing a sawbench it does pay to establish just what can be adjusted, and what cannot. In this connection it is worth noting that where tilting facilities are provided for table or blade, there should be adjustable stops to facilitate replacement of the table or blade in its normal position, so that complete accuracy can be maintained.

The actual processes of cutting are described later, but it is essential to have a good understanding of the machine itself, and its accessories, not least important of which are the blade guard and the riving knife. These two items are of great importance in terms of safety, and on the majority of sawbenches they are joined together, the top of the riving knife being the attachment point for the guard.

The Blade Guard

The purpose of the guard, fairly obviously, is to prevent accidental contact between hand and saw teeth, and a well designed one will do this at all times when the machine is in use. This was not always so, and some very dubious guards have been manufactured in the past. The law is now very strict about such matters, and quite rightly so, as a result of which there has been a great improvement. In England it is illegal to sell machinery which does not conform to safety regulations, and the wise worker uses guards at all times. Occasionally these can be a nuisance, but a nuisance is infinitely preferable to an injury.

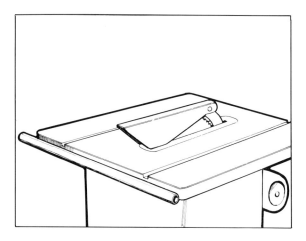

A typical sawguard, attached to top of riving knife, for use when cutting right through the timber. The guard is shaped so that it is lifted by the wood, on which it rests during the cut.

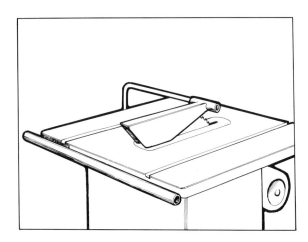

Circular saw blades must always be guarded. With this type of guard the riving knife can be removed so the timber is not obstructed when cutting housing joints etc.

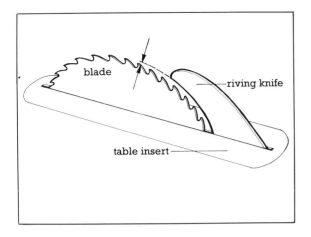

The gap between riving knife and teeth of blade must not be greater than advised by makers. Normally this is about $\frac{1}{8}$ inch.

The Riving Knife

The essential purpose of a riving knife is to prevent closure of the saw kerf when timber is being ripped. If this occurs, the back of the blade is pinched by the timber, causing tearing of the sawn surface, or burning of the wood and heating of the blade if the kerf closes tightly. A riving knife should always be used when ripping, but is not needed in cross-cut operations. It will, however, be necessary for the riving knife to be in position when cross-cutting if it provides the attachment point for the guard.

Rebating and Cutting Joints

In the case of cuts which do not pass right through the timber, as in rebating, or cutting joints, the riving knife cannot be used, as will be clear after a study of the drawings. On many machines this means that the guard cannot be used either, since it fits to the riving knife. For home users, work of this nature is a frequent requirement, therefore an alternative form of guard is advisable. It may be possible to purchase a suitable one as an optional extra, or to have one made locally. Guards used for work of this nature are suspended above the blade by

means of an arm, which is attached to the rear or to one side of the table.

Blades

Various types of sawblade can be obtained for small sawbenches, but it is not necessary for the home worker to delve deeply into the theoretical aspects of sawblade manufacture and design, or tooth angles. Blades designed specifically for ripping along the grain do not crosscut well, and crosscut blades do not rip well, but there are general purpose or 'combination' blades. These represent a compromise, and when sharp and correctly set they are reasonably efficient in both operations, and are the type normally supplied with new machines.

Modern woodworking will, in many cases, involve the cutting of plywood, chipboard, and other resin bonded materials. These will blunt an ordinary carbon steel blade in a very short time, therefore when man-made board is likely to be cut frequently, a TCT blade is advisable. The initials stand for 'tungsten carbide tipped', and blades of this type are expensive. The blade itself is of steel, only the actual teeth being of tungsten carbide, and the cost of such a blade will depend upon the number of teeth it carries. TCT blades will run efficiently for long periods between sharpenings, but they cannot be sharpened in the home workshop because special machinery is required.

Safety Points

The arch enemy of the sawyer is the hidden nail or screw, which can ruin a sawblade. Such items are hardly to be expected in new timber, but they do lurk in reclaimed wood such as dismantled furniture, or timber purchased from demolition firms. The most effective answer to the problem is a small metal detector, of the type often advertised in woodworking magazines.

Dust is another enemy, and quite large quantities are produced when sawbenches are in use. A dust mask should be worn, although the best answer is a good dust extractor, such as the De Walt.

USING THE SAWBENCH

Ripping

This operation is sometimes referred to as rip-sawing, and consists of cutting right through a workpiece along its length. The rip fence guides the wood, which is kept firmly in contact with the fence throughout the cut. The surface which rides against the fence, and the one which contacts the table, must be straight and true. A wobbly edge cannot guide the wood along the fence, and if the timber is not flat on the table it may suddenly twist and jam the blade.

For efficient and safe working, the saw teeth should only just emerge through the upper surface of the wood, so the first step is to set the machine to achieve this. The rip fence is then positioned so that the required width of timber will be cut, either by using a scale which may be provided on the machine, or by physical measurement with a rule, which is the method preferred by most sawyers. The measurement must be from a tooth which leans in towards the fence, sliding the fence along its mounting bar, and locking it in place with locking screw when it is correctly located. Some machines have a fine screw feed adjuster, which is helpful but not essential. Note that when adjustments are made to machinery, the plug should be removed from the electrical socket. Simply switching off is not an adequate safeguard.

Some timber will open when being ripped, rather than try to close on the back of the blade. If the rip fence is long, this can create inaccuracy because the wood pushes itself away from the fence. The problem can be overcome by fitting a piece of wood to the rip fence, the end of the wood being just past the front of the blade.

The safe and efficient ripping of timber soon becomes second nature, but the correct procedure must be adopted from the start. Ripping, especially on thick wood, takes a lot of power, so the feed rate of wood to blade must be steady, enabling the motor to keep up its speed. Both hands are used at the start of a rip cut on reasonably long wood, and many workers like to hook a couple of fingers over

the rip fence to anchor the hand. The wood must be fully supported by both table and fence, and cuts of this kind should always be completed with the aid of a push stick.

Safety

Statistics show the back of a circular sawblade to be more dangerous than the front, for two

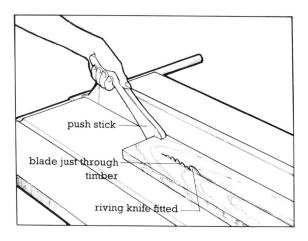

When ripping timber, a push stick should be used to complete the cut.

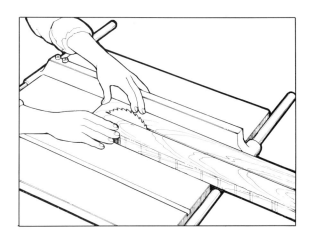

Finishing a rip cut by hand, as here, is highly dangerous. Always use a push stick.

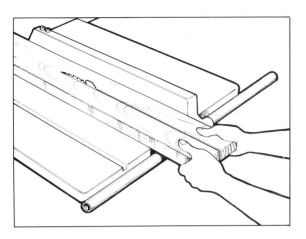

Timber can be ripped partway, then pulled through from rear of machine – not easy at first, but the knack is soon acquired.

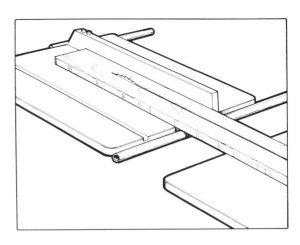

Long workpieces should not be ripped right through without some support.

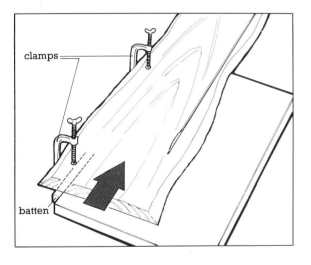

A batten clamped under an irregular board can be run against the saw table edge to produce a straight cut.

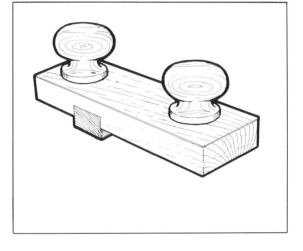

Pusher block for use with circular saws and planers. Handles can be bought, or turned on a wood lathe. This protects the worker's hands as the wood is held down and fed to the blade or cutters.

reasons. Firstly it is rising from the table surface, and will therefore lift the wood if it can. Secondly if a hand is behind the blade, it may be brought into contact with the teeth in the event of a kick-back. If the riving knife and guard are in place, they will help in such a situation, but it is best to keep hands forward of the blade.

When long workpieces are ripped it is essential to establish before starting the cut that nothing will impede the passage of the timber, and which handling method is to be adopted. If the wood is of reasonable length, the cut is completed with a push stick, and the wood tips up as

the blade emerges, remaining trapped by the guard, or on some machines it may simply fall off the rear edge of the table onto the floor. With very long pieces, however, the weight of the timber projecting over the back of the table increases as the cut proceeds, and an element of danger is introduced, because the work becomes increasingly difficult to control.

Where a lot of long ripping is envisaged, it is worth making a support roller which can be positioned behind the machine. If the sawbench is of the rise and fall table variety, the roller support will have to be adjustable in height, but if it is the blade which moves rather than the table, this facility will not be required.

Where space is a problem it may be better to use the system of ripping a little over halfway through the workpiece, then withdrawing the wood and turning it end for end, completing the cut with the same side against the fence.

Yet another approach with long work is the pull through method, which is quite safe, but can require a little practice before the wood can be kept easily against the fence. This is simply a matter of walking to the rear of the machine and pulling the work through the second half of its travel, keeping the hands well clear of the blade.

Resawing

Resawing is another ripping operation, but is best avoided by beginners, since it is quite dangerous unless carried out correctly. The idea is to cut timber through edgewise along its length, to produce two thin boards from one thick specimen. This procedure can produce apprehension in quite competent people, and is best left well alone.

Rebating and Groove Cutting

Two further operations which involve use of the rip fence are rebating and the cutting of grooves. Both can be performed with a standard sawblade, but where much work of this nature is called for a dado or wobble saw (see p. 140) will save considerable time. Grooving with a sawblade consists of making one cut to the required depth along the wood, then repeating the process as many times as necessary, moving the rip fence by the width of a saw kerf between each cut. A dado head or wobble saw can usually be set to complete the groove in one pass.

Rebating can be done with these accessories, but where the rebates are large it may be worth saving the strips which are produced by rebating with two saw cuts. A rebate might be described as a groove along the edge of the wood, so it could be produced with a sawblade as described above. Frequently, however, it is better to make two saw cuts, one from the face and one from the edge, which meet and remove a length of wood. The marking out of the timber and setting of the fence for each cut must be done carefully, and the edge cut should be

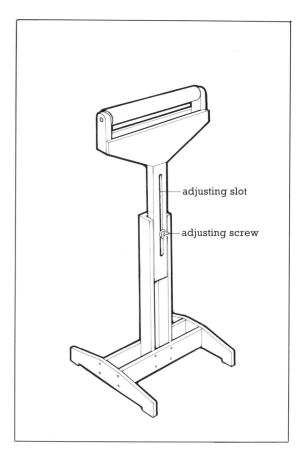

Suggestion for a home-made roller take-off for long work ripped on a circlar saw, dimensions to suit the machine in use. It need only be made adjustable if used with rise and fall table saws.

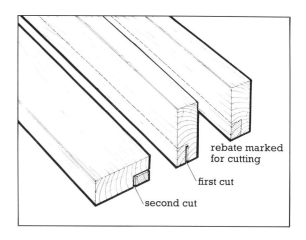

Two sawcuts remove a strip of wood to form a rebate. Cuts should be made in order shown to provide maximum support during second cut.

made first, so that the wood retains adequate support. When the second cut is performed, into the face of the wood, the waste strip may be ejected violently as the cut is completed, so it is as well to stand to one side.

Sawtable Inserts

The sawtable insert is a section of metal, plastic, or wood, which immediately surrounds the blade, and must be removed when fitting dado heads, wobble saws, or moulding blocks. When very thin material has to be ripped from a workpiece, as in the production of mouldings, or strips for edging purposes, a home-made plywood insert is fitted. This is made without a slot for the sawblade, and when it has been screwed firmly in position the machine is started and the blade brought up to cut its own slot. This provides support right up to the blade, and prevents thin work from being dragged down by the saw.

Crosscutting

Crosscutting, as the name suggests, consists of cutting wood across its grain, the most common requirement being a cut at ninety degrees to the edge. A mitre guide of some kind is used, either sliding in a slot cut in the sawtable, or running on a bar fixed to the side of the machine. It is therefore imperative that the table be parallel to the blade, and the mitre guide set exactly at the required angle, with its clamping screw tight. Many mitre guides have an adjustable stop for the ninety degree position, which should be checked and adjusted as required with the aid of a carpenter's square.

All work being machined must be fully supported by the table and by the guide or fence, and crosscutting is no exception to this. Where safety is concerned the golden rule is 'if in doubt, don't'.

Mitre Guides

Mitre guides can be used in their standard form, as supplied with the sawbench, but their value is greatly enhanced by the addition of home-made sub-fences, as shown in the illustrations. These can increase both safety and accuracy, since they provide more support for the workpiece, and can be extremely helpful where numerous pieces of equal length are required. The type which is slotted to accept a bolt and wing nut which can secure a stop block

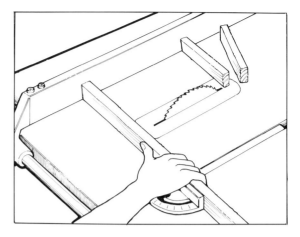

The rip fence should NEVER be used as a stop when cutting small pieces to length. The off cuts can be rejected with great force.

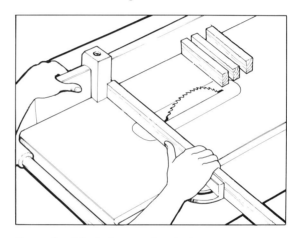

A wooden block fixed to the rip fence forward of the blade can be used as a length stop when crosscutting. Severed pieces cannot then jam between the blade and fence.

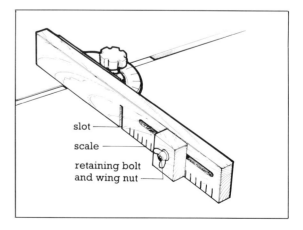

Adjustable stop block for repetition crosscutting to length. The wooden sub fence can be made to any desired length.

31

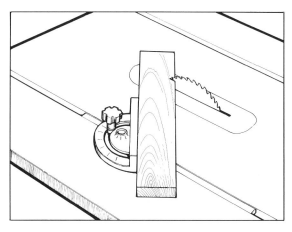

Mitre guide used in 'closed' position. Workpieces can be clamped to the mitre guide if desired.

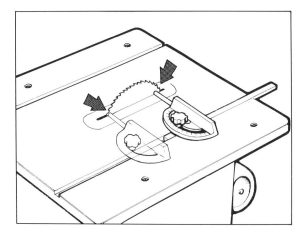

The blade must be exactly parallel to the mitre guide slots. This can be checked as shown here, by means of a rod held against the guide.

is the best, and if desired a yardstick can be let into the face of the fence. The simpler type, without a sliding block, is also useful, but both types need to be high enough to be drastically weakened (or even cut through) when the saw is at full projection. Stop blocks should not touch the table, a gap being left so that dust and chips will not accumulate and interfere with accuracy. A stop block is not essential, since when the first cut has been made with a sub-fence measurements can be taken from the resulting kerf, and work aligned to a pencil mark on the fence.

Work being crosscut must be held firmly to the guide, which is used to push it forward. The section which is being cut off should not be held, since this achieves nothing, and is likely to result in a kick back if forward pressure is being applied as the cut ends. Small offcuts have inherent dangers on many machines, and must not be touched until the saw is stationary, nor should they be allowed to accumulate on the table. Experienced workers remove such pieces by pushing them off the table with the aid of a piece of scrap wood, but when the sawing operations are completed these scraps should be swept up and the floor around the machine left clean. It is also dangerous to crosscut very short pieces of timber, which necessarily brings the hands far too close to the blade. If such operations really must be carried out the work should be clamped firmly to the fence and the hands kept well clear.

Most sawbenches provide some means of reversing the mitre guide so that it faces towards the operator. This facility is designed to permit the crosscutting of wide material, where the width of the workpiece precludes any possibility of normal mitre guide use. In these cases the wood is still held firmly to the guide, but the work now pushes the guide forward.

Note that when long pieces require crosscutting at some point near their centres, there exists a danger of the wood sagging towards the end of the operation, due to its projection over the edge of the table. If this occurs, the wood may pinch the sawblade, and so produce a kick back. Some form of support should be provided for the ends of the wood in such cases, and it may be found easier to use a hand saw initially, trimming precisely on the sawbench afterwards.

The crosscutting of wood which is thicker than the capacity of the machine is similar to the ripping of such stock, in that a cut is made to a little more than halfway, the wood then being turned over and the job completed. If the edges of the wood are not known to be parallel, the same side of the workpiece should contact the fence for each cut.

Freehand crosscutting should be avoided, it is bad practice, though often done by experienced sawyers. If the wood is twisted while doing this, or if both ends of the wood are being pushed, there is every chance of a kick back.

Mitre Cuts

The word 'mitre' is frequently thought by beginners to be a reference to the cutting of wood at an angle of forty five degrees, since they associate the term with picture frames. In fact a mitre is an angled cut across a workpiece, the specific angle being irrelevant, and the operation is a form of crosscutting. The scale provided on the mitre guide can be used for general mitring, but where a high degree of accuracy is required it is better to make special templates from plywood or hardboard, which can be positioned against the fence and the guide rotated until the template registers exactly with the blade, the guide then being clamped tight, and a test cut made in scrap material.

Some mitre cuts are made with the guide at an angle other than ninety degrees to the blade, and the blade or table tilted. These are known as compound mitres, and a check should be made before switching on to ensure that the blade cannot contact the mitre fence during the cut. If the front face of the guide forms an obtuse angle with the blade, the guide is described as being in the open position. If the angle is acute the position is referred to as closed.

If precautions are not taken, the material may move slightly along the guide fence during the cut, this being known as 'creep', and the movement is usually towards the blade. It can be prevented by using a sub-fence with a few nail or screw points protruding slightly from it to grip the wood, or by fixing a strip of coarse abrasive paper to the face of the guide by means of ad-

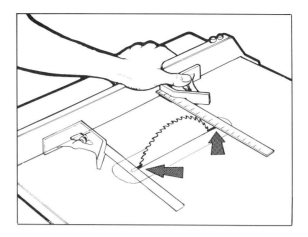

The rip fence must be set parallel to the blade when the blade has been aligned with the mitre guide slot.

hesive. If creep occurs there is likely to be slight bowing of the cut face of the workpiece.

It is important to be quite certain at all times when using a mitre guide that the clamping screw is really tight, and that there is no danger of the guide swinging on its pivot during the cut. The rate of feed of the wood to the blade should be steady, and the movement smooth.

Making a Jig

Mitre guides can be quite useful items, but they are frequently quite pitiful objects as supplied with cheap sawbenches, and for precise work most sawyers make jigs which will ensure ac-

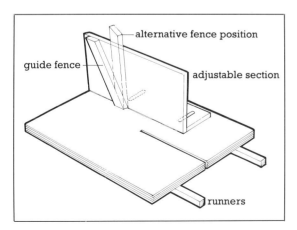

A jig for slotting ends of timber to take plywood splines, easily made in the workshop.

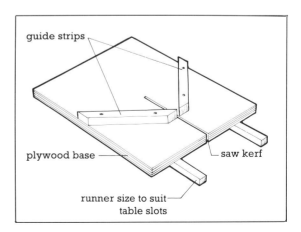

A home-made mitring jig for a circular saw. Work is positioned against one of the guide fences and moved forward with the jig to the saw blade.

curacy, and which obviate the need to swing the guide on its pivot when changing from a left hand to a right hand mitre. These are not at all difficult to make, and well worth the time and trouble. Care in the making will pay dividends, however, so the job should be done slowly. The sketches will help to explain the construction of such jigs, and it will be noted that when mitring on the inside of the runners the edge of the wood is against one of them, and the end against the other, which effectively prevents creep from occurring.

The illustrations show how such jigs are constructed, and there is no real problem in making one, but it is of course vital that the angle between each of the small fences and the blade is exactly forty five degrees if the jig is for picture frames, and equal precision is required for any other angle. There will be either one or two runners fitted to the underside of the jig, depending upon how many mitre guide slots the table has, and the simplest method of fitting these is to prepare them as precise fits in the guide slots of the table, place them in the slots

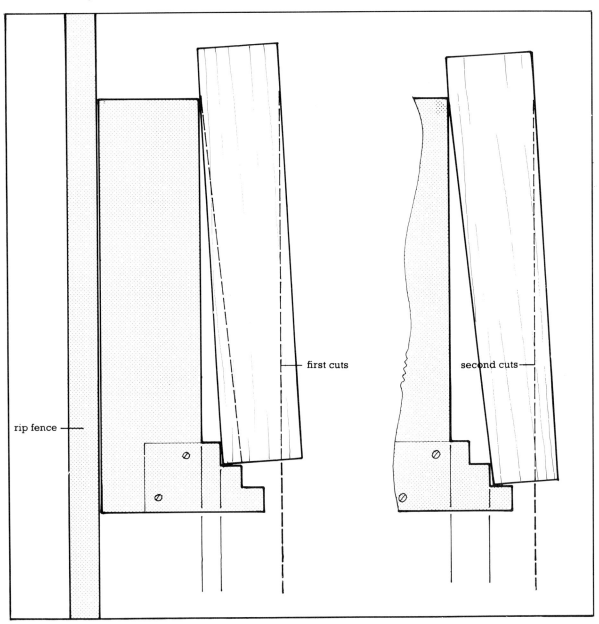

first cuts

rip fence

second cuts

A stepped jig for taper sawing. For tapered square legs cuts are made on two adjacent sides with wood in first notch, and remaining sides are cut with wood in second notch. Wood and jig slide forward together along rip fence.

34

and apply adhesive to their upper surfaces, then put the main board carefully in position on them and leave it under some form of weight until the glue has set. The runners can then be drilled, countersunk to accept screw heads, and screwed firmly in place. The board can be three eighths to half an inch thick, and it must be truly flat, which is not always the case even with man-made board. A fine toothed crosscut pattern blade will work well if sharp, but a TCT blade with a large number of teeth can be substituted.

The next stage is the cutting of the slot in the board, which can be done by advancing the board on its runners into the rotating blade. The saw is then switched off, and the upper guides are installed, with great care. The jig's accuracy is dependent upon this operation, so it must not be rushed. I use impact adhesive to position the two strips of wood along lines which I mark with a protractor and a sharp pen-

cil, since this type of adhesive permits minute alterations as the strips are finally screwed in place. When the jig is complete, it will be as well to make up a small frame and check it for accuracy, or at least to make a ninety degree assembly from two pieces cut on the jig and check them with a square. The big advantage with most jigs is that once they are proved to be accurate, they can be relied upon to remain so.

Workpieces which are to be mitred other than at the end can be positioned against the outside of the guide strips, but note that creep is now possible.

Maintenance

Items which seem to cause considerable confusion among beginners are the types of circular sawblade, and the various accessories such as dado heads, wobble saws, and moulding blocks. It is not my intention to go deeply into

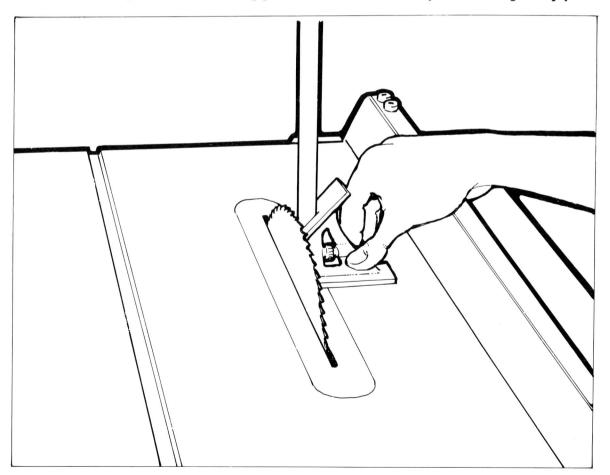

The blade is checked and set at 90° to the table, then the pointer is set to zero on the tilt scale. The square must be placed against a tooth which leans away from it.

the question of sawblade care, but only to describe those aspects which are likely to concern the home user. The hobbyist does, however, need to know what types of blade will be of use in the home workshop, and to have some idea of what can reasonably be attempted in the field of blade maintenance. It is also worth noting that dado heads and wobble saws are expensive, and unless there is likely to be a constant call for them in the cutting of woodworking joints, rebates, and grooves, an ordinary blade can do the job quite well.

Blades

The best quality blades are not cheap, but cheap blades should be avoided, since they are likely to prove expensive in the long term. It is better to have just one, or perhaps two good blades than a collection of dubious objects, and there is no doubt that clever advertising does promote the sale of sawblades which are hardly ever used. Since man-made board of various types is now freely available, and the resin bonding of these materials will blunt ordinary steel blades very quickly indeed, many workers now use one TCT blade almost exclusively, and manage very well. The edges of tungsten carbide teeth will keep their sharpness up to a hundred times longer than their steel counterparts, but cheap TCT blades must be shunned, because they are usually made from inferior grades of tungsten carbide, and will perform accordingly. The best advice I can offer is that the best quality blade which can be afforded should be purchased, and looked after carefully. The teeth of these blades are brittle, and will chip if knocked by another piece of metal, or dropped onto a metal surface. The best ones come in wooden boxes, and should be kept there when not in use.

Before looking at the different types of blade, it is worth noting some general points. The gullets, or gaps between the teeth, have a specific job to do, which consists of collecting the chippings as the teeth pass through the wood, and ejecting them with the aid of centrifugal force when the teeth emerge. They therefore have to be maintained in the correct shape and at the proper depth, and must not be allowed to become blocked with hardened resin, which can happen if a lot of softwood is cut. If the teeth are blunt, or the gullets are not doing their job, the blade will be heated by friction beyond acceptable limits. When a new blade is purchased it is worth drawing round it carefully with a sharp pencil to give a reference on paper to the original shape.

The outer part of a sawblade is subjected to friction and some degree of heat when cutting, and so some expansion occurs, but since the central part remains cool there can be distortion. Steel sawblades are 'tensioned' by a hammering process during manufacture, and if found to be out of true, so that they can be seen to wobble when turned slowly by hand, must be sent to a saw doctor for attention. In the case of TCT blades, expansion is catered for by means of slots in the blade itself, which terminate in circular apertures. Note also that no sawblade can be expected to perform well if it is not an exact fit on the spindle of the machine, either because the hole in the blade is enlarged, or due to wear having produced a groove in the spindle.

Types of Blade

The normal type of steel blade is relatively cheap, works well, and is quite satisfactory if kept sharp. The patterns of most interest to home users are the rip, crosscut, and combination blades.

Rip blades are rather wicked looking objects to the uninitiated, since they have fewer and larger teeth than other types, but they will do their job safely and efficiently if properly maintained. When used for crosscutting they do the job, but the finish is rougher than would be the case with a crosscut blade. The teeth of a rip blade have a definite hooked appearance.

Crosscut blades carry a large number of small triangular teeth, which must be sharpened with care, and the process can take quite a long time on a ten or twelve inch diameter blade. The sharpening is not, however, particularly difficult.

Combination blades are a compromise. They do not rip or crosscut quite as well as blades designed specifically for these operations, but they give very acceptable results in most general woodworking, and are widely used.

Maintenance of Blades

Saw maintenance operations which can be undertaken by home users are described below, and the normal system is to keep blades in reasonable condition by these methods for as long as possible, but to let them have a full service from a saw doctor when really necessary. The cost of sending a blade to an expert every time it needs sharpening is prohibitive, quite apart from the inconvenience of being without it for some time.

A blade which needs attention should first be checked for precise fit on the spindle, then reversed on the spindle and the retaining nut replaced. The teeth are now pointing backwards. This is in preparation for an operation known by various names, 'ranging' or 'topping' being quite commonly employed. The point is that the tips of all teeth should be exactly the same distance from the saw spindle, so that all teeth will do the same amount of work when cutting. A smooth block of hardwood is now placed on the table directly over the blade, and the depth control is used to set the machine so that the saw teeth are just touching the wood, the table or blade then being securely clamped. The machine is then started, and a coarse oilstone or a disused grinding wheel is placed flat on the table and moved forward until the teeth just touch it for a few seconds. The machine is then switched off, and the blade examined to establish whether or not all teeth have been marked by the stone. This is unlikely at this stage, so the saw is given a tiny fraction more projection, and the process is repeated. Several passes may be required, but when every tooth has been marked the job is done.

The process is not difficult if carried out carefully, but those of a nervous disposition may prefer to remove the plug from the wall socket and turn the blade by hand, which will take more time, and is awkward on some machines, but presents no danger.

Teeth

The teeth can now be set, the expression 'set' being a reference to the outward lean of the top third of a saw tooth, each tooth leaning the opposite way to those on either side. Set gives a kerf, or saw cut, which is wider than the blade itself, allowing the blade to run free so that it does not bind in the cut and become overheated. Special tools can be obtained for this purpose, accuracy being very important. These tools are known as 'setting pliers', and are not cheap. The set is very slight, and will not normally exceed $\frac{1}{64}$ inch.

A sawblade vice can be constructed from oddments of wood, and will be found very useful,

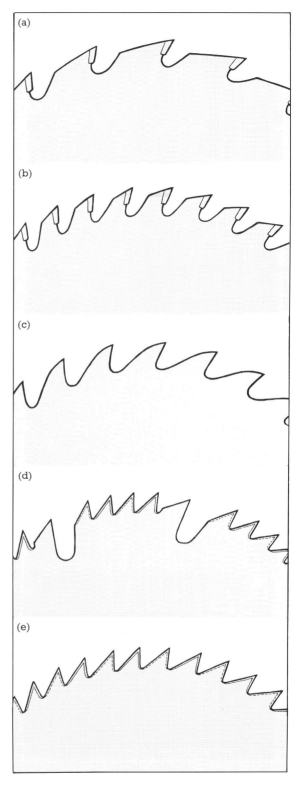

(a) and (b). Tungsten carbide tipped blades have teeth which are extremely hard, but also brittle and easily damaged by rough handling.
(c) (d) and (e) Saw tooth patterns: (c) rip; (d) novelty or planer; (e) combination.

37

but I have not found a sophisticated type to be necessary, and merely sandwich my blades between two wooden discs in the vice when sharpening. For rip blades a mill file is used. This has a convex edge which can be employed for a clean up of the gullet, the flat part of the file being used to sharpen the teeth. The original angle across the tooth must be maintained, and those unused to filing may find it helpful to blacken all the teeth in the smoke from a candle which has a long wick. Care must be exercised here, to avoid any overheating, but the soot will show whether or not the first file stroke is flat on the metal, and any correction required is easily made. Each tooth is filed until the last speck of soot has gone, but no more than this. The tops of rip teeth are filed, but the fronts are best left alone.

If teeth which lean towards the worker are filed there will be judder, which spoils the process, so those which lean away are done first, the blade then being turned round to complete the operation. If the work has been done properly, the blade should now perform very well indeed, but the gullets do become shallower with each sharpening, and will eventually need to be recut by a saw doctor. The filing of crosscut teeth is time consuming, but well worth the effort. A small triangular file is used for this, and one or two strokes per tooth should be sufficient.

TCT blades cannot be sharpened at home, and they have no set, which is unnecessary because the teeth are wider than the thickness of the blade.

PORTABLE CIRCULAR SAWS

The hand held portable saw, with its integral motor, is a useful device where it is necessary for a powered saw to be taken to the site of the job. For occasional use around the home and garden these machines will serve quite well, but many workers will require more accurate and sophisticated equipment, which is also readily portable. The descriptions which follow are of two extremely interesting circular saws, both manufactured by Elu, which fulfil these requirements admirably.

The saws in question are the PS174, and the TGS172, both of which can easily be moved from room to room for operations such as the construction of built-in furniture, or transported in a car by those who need to work away from home. These tools have certain basic similarities, but they are in fact widely divergent in design, and merit individual discussion.

The PS174

The PS174, unlike the TGS172, is not designed for ripping timber along its length. It is essentially a 'cut-off' saw, designed to deal with relatively narrow crosscut operations, with provision for accurate angle cutting. Machines of the

Small portable circular saws of this kind are extremely useful for home maintenance, and for cutting large sheets of man-made board to manageable sizes before processing them on larger workshop machinery. These saws are quite safe provided that the guard can move freely on its pivot, and so will return immediately to cover the blade at the end of a cut.

'cut-off' or 'snipper' variety have the saw unit complete with motor attached to the rear of the sawtable, and when at rest the saw unit is held above the table by a return spring. There is a slot in the table, into which the blade passes when the saw unit is pulled downwards by the operator, against the spring pressure. The material to be cut is positioned against a fence at the rear of the table, and held firmly as the cut is made.

Most saws of this nature can only deal with quite narrow workpieces, but the advantage offered by the PS174 is that it has a telescoping arm feature. When the saw has been pulled down and cut into the wood, it can be drawn towards the front of the table, and when the cut is completed the blade will be lifted clear of the wood as the operator releases the downward pressure.

Both saws under discussion here have excellent guard systems, and are probably as safe as it is possible to make them, but it is important with snipper saws, as with radial arms, to ensure that the timber is firmly against the fence before it contacts the blade.

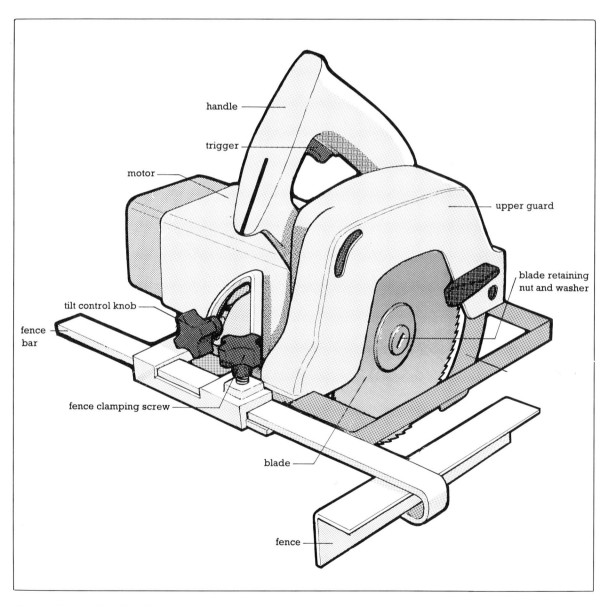

A typical portable electric circular saw.

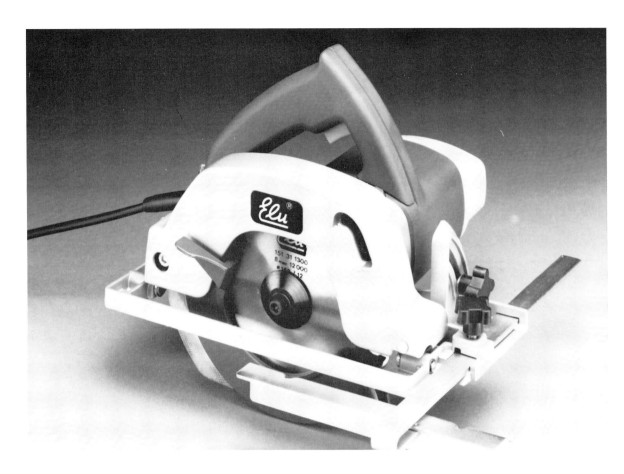

A portable circular saw with rip fence and tilt mechanism for bevel ripping.

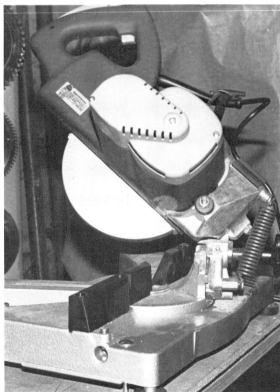

Long trigger in top of handle swings guard back in readiness for cutting, small trigger below operates motor. These saws are extremely well designed and made.

Elu PS174 circular saw, in ninety degree cut-off mode. Note heavy duty return spring at rear, and radial angle selection system at front, with notches for commonly used angles.

Construction of the PS174

The PS174 is attached to the rear of the table by a pivot mechanism, which is also designed to permit tilting of the saw head unit. In its normal position, for square cut-off work, the blade will be at a ninety degree angle to both fence and table surface. When a clamping device at the base of the saw unit is released, the saw head can be tilted to present the blade at angles other than ninety degrees to the table surface, the desired angle being read from a scale and the clamp tightened. Accuracy here will of course depend upon the scale reading zero when the blade is perpendicular, so this should be checked, and the pointer adjusted as necessary. When tilted in this manner, the saw can perform bevelled crosscuts, such as might be required for the components of shallow boxes with mitred corners.

Angled crosscutting is also possible, and the setting of the required angle is a simple procedure. A small clamp is released at the front of the table, and a latch is lifted. This permits the saw head unit to rotate on its mounting pin to provide the required angle, which can be at any one of a number of pre-set positions, where the latch locates positively in a notch, or at intermediate points selected from a scale. Combined use of the tilting and radial swing facilities will therefore permit the setting of compound angles, where the blade is at an angle other than ninety degrees both through and across the wood.

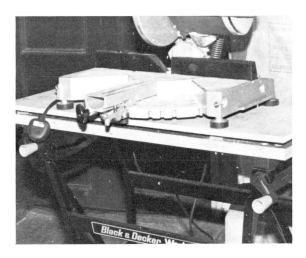

PS174 mounted firmly in Workmate. Both items are readily portable, and are therefore an excellent combination. Sawblade guarding is fully efficient.

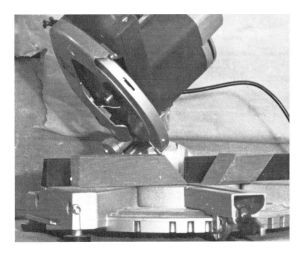

Saw head can be tilted by means of a control at the rear, to provide a facility for angled cuts through the timber. Tilt can be combined with radial swing, to give compound angles.

Safety

The PS174 is fully guarded, as the illustrations show, the guard being swung clear by the operation of a trigger as the cut commences. Timber to be cut is placed against the fence, and MUST lie flat against both fence and table surface, or it may move during the cut and jam the blade.

A TCT blade is fitted as standard, and this produces a smooth sawn surface.

Use

When cutting narrow stock it is merely necessary to swing the head down until the blade has severed the wood. If the wood is wider, however, the saw is pulled down through it, then drawn forward towards the operator, and boards up to approximately ten inches in width can be crosscut. The width of board which can be cut will be less when the blade is not cutting at ninety degrees across the material, since the limiting factor is the possible travel of the saw head on the telescopic arms.

This machine is not heavy, and can be carried around by anyone with normal health and strength.

The TGS172

The TGS172 is a different creature, and is likely to have much wider appeal among home woodworkers. An ingenious and highly efficient design feature permits the tool to be used as a cut-off saw for straight or angled work, or as a very useful sawbench. When in cut-off mode the saw differs from the PS172 in that it does not have the pull through facility, and so cannot deal with such wide boards. It is, on the other hand, very useful for accurate cut-off work, and can be employed for cuts at various angles to its fence and/or table. Its big attraction is its ability to be converted simply and rapidly into a sawbench.

Changing from one mode to the other takes only a few moments, and is achieved by pivoting the saw unit and table in its frame. When set up as a sawbench it is extremely efficient, and performs more than adequately with the TCT blade provided.

As the illustrations show, the machine has a rip fence, mitre guide, depth control, and a very effective guard, which in the sawbench mode

attaches to the riving knife. This machine is also portable. Its four strong tubular legs can be fitted or removed in a few moments, and it will fit easily into most cars for transportation from site to site.

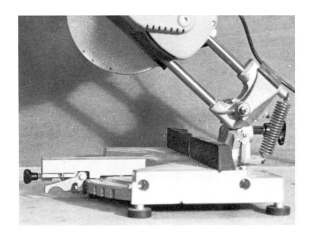

Showing the telescoping arms of the PS174, which enable it to cut wider boards. Tilt control knob can be seen behind the return spring.

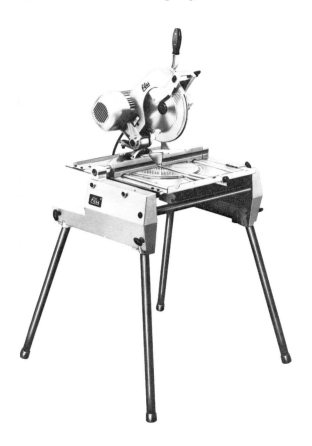

The TGS 172 saw mounted on detachable tubular legs.

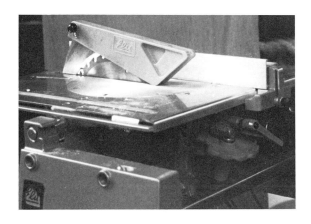

Elu TGS172 dual purpose saw in sawbench mode. Rip fence is shown in forward position relative to its mounting point.

The table is pivoted in the frame to bring the machine into cut-off mode.

Here the guard has been raised to show the riving knife, and the fence has been slid forward. Note depth of cut control, centre right.

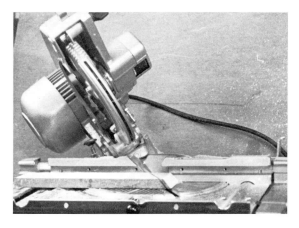

Here shown in cut-off mode, the tool has just completed a compound angled cut.

Completing a rip cut with a push stick on the TGS172.

The saw is pulled smoothly down through the wood, and returns to its original position by the influence of the return spring at rear.

5

THE RADIAL ARM SAW

The first name that comes to mind when radial arm saws are mentioned is undoubtedly De Walt, which is hardly surprising since the first De Walt model was put on the market in 1922. There have been many models over the years, each incorporating improvements or extending the capabilities as technology has progressed. There have also been challenges from other manufacturers, but these have been about as successful as the various attempts to produce a vehicle which would destroy the supremacy of the ubiquitous Land Rover. In view of the vast number of these saws which are in constant use around the world, it is necessary to point out that if they are cared for they have a very long life, which presents a slight problem when one begins to write a chapter about them. There are minor differences between the models, so that the precise positions and shapes of controls, locking levers, saw guards, and the like do vary. The functions of these items however remain the same, so allowance should be made if readers find that the illustrations differ from machines they have examined.

Students who visit my workshop for woodturning or machinery familiarisation courses often exhibit interest in the two De Walts, and ask what they are capable of. I have a small version which has served me well for some fourteen years, and a monster 'builder's model', which is a few months old. Unfortunately, as is the case with routers, it is really quicker to explain what they will not do, since what can be done by a skilled man with the basic machine and a few attachments is almost incredible. This is a pity in a way, because some people feel that highly versatile machines are too complicated for

them. The basic functions of a radial arm saw are not difficult to comprehend, and although it may take a while to become completely at home with the tool, the time and effort are certain to pay rich dividends. The purpose of this chapter is to explain the construction, capabilities, and techniques of safe and efficient use of this fascinating piece of equipment. In my view a radial is a safer tool in the hands of a beginner than a sawbench, and will definitely offer more scope in general woodworking terms.

Not least among the many advantages offered by radial arm saws is the fact that they can be positioned against a wall, whereas a sawbench needs to be somewhere in the centre of the

De Walt 8001 radial arm saw. This model is larger than the home user 'Powershop' models, but essentially similar. The tool is compact, efficient, and versatile.

workshop, because timber which is being ripped on a sawbench is passed from front to rear. Ripping on the radial is done either from left to right or vice versa, as will be explained later, and little or no space is required at the rear of the machine. Another point which appeals to users is that when cutting grooves, housings, or joints, where the blade does not pass right through the material, the radial is fully guarded, and the layout marks on the timber are uppermost, rather than against the table surface and out of sight, as is the case with a sawbench. The dreaded 'kick back', so feared by many novices with circular saws, is also far less likely to occur.

Construction

The basic components of a radial arm saw are a metal base at the rear of which a heavy duty steel cylinder is mounted centrally in the vertical plane. The arm from which the machine derives its name is attached to the top of the column in the horizontal plane, and a motor is mounted in a yoke below the arm. The yoke in which the motor is mounted gives the machine considerable versatility, and the fact that the arm can be moved radially on the column enhances this. The motor in fact can be rotated in the horizontal plane in its yoke, and can be tilted in the vertical plane.

The arm, and with it of course the motor, can be raised or lowered relative to the base of the machine, by means of a control which is unfortunately situated on top of the column. Attempts have been made to provide a control 'up front' within easy reach, but unless these are of a heavy duty nature they eventually fail, and if they are suitably heavy they make the machine too expensive. One does become accustomed to this, however, and it is merely a minor irritation.

Assembly

Some assembly operations are necessary when a new machine is delivered to the workshop, and these must be carried out carefully, in exact accordance with the instructions provided by the manufacturer. A table, made of a high density particle board, is provided, and must be fixed to the base so that it is level in relation to the travel of the motor. This takes time, but is quite easy. The end cap must be removed from the arm, so that the motor can be fitted, the roller bearings on the motor being slid into tracks

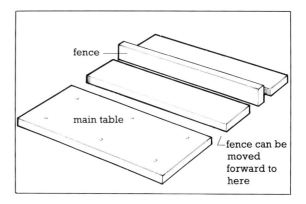

De Walt radial arm saw tables are composed of three horizontal sections and a vertical fence, which is pinched between the horizontal boards by thumbscrews at rear.

on the underside of the arm. The end cap must be replaced so that it is held firmly in position. Various checks are then carried out, as described in the instructions, and the machine is ready for use once its sawblade and guard have been fitted. The fence is also of particle board, but can be replaced when necessary by a hardwood or softwood version of the same thickness. It is fixed in place by inserting it edgewise between the main or front part of the table, and two narrow sections at the rear, pressure being applied by means of two clamping devices at the back of the machine. All the machines shown in this book will run with a normal three pin plug inserted into a thirteen amp socket, but if the cable should ever require replacement it is important to ensure that the new cable is of the same specification as the old one.

The guards now fitted to De Walt radials are rather complicated by comparison with those found on sawbenches, but they are very efficient, and under no circumstances should the saw be used without them.

Position of Motor

Provided that the maker's instructions have been followed completely and faithfully, the machine should now be ready for use, but one important safety point arises here. This is that when not cutting, the motor should always be parked at the rear of the arm, so that the sawblade is behind the fence. One develops the habit of returning it to this position, but there is a special device which can be fitted to De Walt saws, which will automatically retract the motor along the arm when the operating handle is released.

One half of dado head fitted to De Walt 8001. Remaining half, with shim washers and retaining nut, is on bench.

Final tightening by means of Allen key, with spanner lodged against sawtable. The cuts produced by the two saw sections always overlap, even with all washers fitted.

Safety return device, at right of picture, below elevating handle, ensures that saw returns to the safe parking area behind the fence after every cut.

Crosscutting

The next step is to switch the machine on, and lower the rotating sawblade until it cuts into the table surface to a depth of about $\frac{1}{16}$ inch. As will be seen, it is necessary for radial saws to cut into the table surface slightly, and those who wish to preserve the table may like to cover it with thin plywood. If this is done, however, great care must be taken to ensure that the plywood is absolutely flat on the table, and that any screws or panel pins are not in an area which the sawblade will cross.

The crosscutting of timber on these saws is a simple matter, the wood being placed firmly against the fence, and the saw pulled along the arm until the cut is complete. One hand holds the timber against the fence, the other operates the saw, and the roles of the hands are interchangeable, the choice being dependent upon convenience. It is very important that the edge of the timber which is placed against the fence is straight, since if this is not the case the wood may move during the cut. The blade should not be pulled through the wood any further than is necessary to complete the cut, otherwise there is a possibility that the offcut may foul the blade as the latter is returned along the arm. The blade will cut a slot in the fence on the first crosscut, and this is subsequently useful for aligning marks on timber which is being cut to length.

View from right of De Walt 8001 shows that blade is fully guarded at all times. Note scale with pointers for in-rip and out-rip operations, fixed along lower edge of arm.

The action of the blade assists in keeping the wood against the fence when crosscutting, but it is as well to check before any such operation that no dust or wood fragments have accumulated against the fence, which could cause inaccuracy. Repetition crosscutting, where a number of pieces are required of the same length, can be done by aligning one end of the wood against a pencil mark on the fence, or by clamping a small block of wood (stop block) to the fence and positioning the wood against this for each cut. Stop blocks of this kind should be just clear of the table surface or sawdust may gather and spoil the accuracy.

Blade Jams

Blunt blades put unnecessary strain on motors, and can also contribute to blade jams, where the blade stalls in the wood. If this occurs the motor should be switched off immediately, and the blade freed from the wood. The usual cause of this phenomenon, which occurs mainly in thicker workpieces, is the saw being pulled too quickly along the arm. A nice steady movement, with no appreciable slowing of the motor, is correct.

Cutting Thick Timber

If timber to be crosscut is thicker than the maximum depth of cut of the saw, the procedure is to set the machine to cut a little more than halfway through the wood, and crosscut in the normal way. The wood is then turned over and a second cut is made, carefully aligning the material so that the first and second cuts meet. Complete success with this method requires the two faces of the wood which are to contact the table to be parallel to each other.

Angled Crosscuts

The most common form of crosscutting is with the blade travelling at ninety degrees to the fence, but the radial arm saw is a very useful machine for angled crosscuts, either at forty five degrees, as required for picture frames, or at other settings. In the case of forty five degree cuts, there is a special setting on the machine, the arm being swung to right or to left until its latch locates. Other settings can be made by reading a scale under the elevating handle, but for very precise work it will be found necessary to construct plywood or hardboard templates to align the blade, and to check the setting again when the locking lever has been tightened.

Preventing 'Creep'

Accuracy in angled crosscutting is not difficult to achieve, but great care must be taken in setting the machine, and some precautions are necessary to prevent the occurrence of a phenomenon known as 'creep'. This is a slight movement of the wood along the fence during the cut, and it can be overcome either by clamping the wood to the fence, or by making and using a special fence which will prevent the timber from moving. This can either be achieved by having the points of a few panel pins protruding from the front face of the fence, or by fixing a strip of coarse abrasive paper to it.

Creep can also occur when cutting bevelled mitres, which are cuts made with the arm at an angle other than ninety degrees, and the motor tilted. These cuts present no special problems, and the tilt scale on the motor mounting will be adequate for most purposes, but it is important to remember to tighten the tilt clamp lever before cutting. Bevelled mitres are not a common requirement in most workshops, but those who, for example, make wooden wheelbarrows (either full size or as toys) will find the radial an excellent tool for the job.

Mitring Fences

Those who need to carry out a fair amount of angled crosscutting may like to invest in a use-

View from left of De Walt 8001, showing the very effective and extremely important blade guard system. Note also chip deflector at upper rear of guard, which ejects chips away from operator.

THE RADIAL ARM SAW

ful accessory which is available for De Walt radials. This consists of a pair of special mitring fences, which can be fitted in place of the standard fence, and can be angled across the table, as the illustration shows. The saw remains in the ninety degree crosscut position, the timber itself being angled relative to the blade by placing it against one or other of the special fences. With this accessory a fresh cut through the standard fence is not produced by each different angle setting, as is the case if the work is done by swinging the saw arm, and a wider range of angles can be achieved. A scale is provided on each fence, and the markings are sufficiently widely spaced to permit accurate setting.

Ripping

The terms 'ripsawing' and 'ripping' refer to cutting timber right through, along its length. When investigated initially, ripping on radial saws can appear to be a complex business, but a radial arm saw will rip timber safely and efficiently if the operator is competent. New owners should, however, ensure that they understand the procedure before attempting to use the machine for this purpose.

There is a choice of two modes for ripping with radials, these being known as 'in rip' and 'out rip'. When in the in rip position, the end of the motor which carries the blade faces the fence, whereas in the out rip position it faces the operator. Under normal circumstances, most ripping is done in the in rip position. It is very important that the wood is fed into the rotation of the sawblade, so the nature of the machine will demand a right to left feed for in ripping, and a feed from left to right when in the out rip mode. All clamps must be checked for tightness before sawing is commenced. The feed is in fact always towards the end of the guard which carries the anti-kick-back fingers and pressure shoe, so there should be no confusion. It is also imperative that the riving knife be in place when ripping, and this would prevent timber from being fed to the saw from the wrong end.

Timber being ripped must have a straight edge against the fence, and is fed forward steadily, but not fast enough to cause a significant drop in r.p.m of the motor. This is hard work for the machine, even with a sharp blade, but there is no cause for alarm if the motor cuts out. An overload protection switch is fitted, and it is merely necessary to leave the machine to cool until it can be reset by means of the reset button.

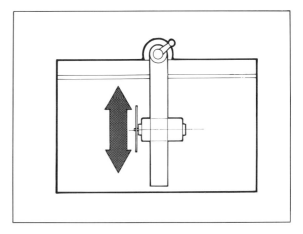

A 90° crosscut.

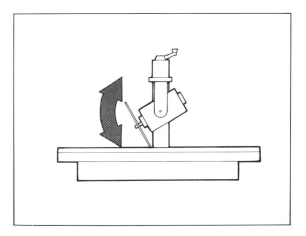

An angled crosscut with the motor tilted.

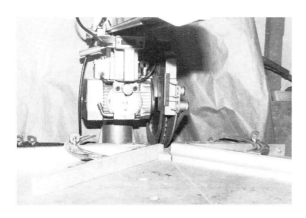

Special mitring fences fitted to De Walt radial arm saw. The pivoting mechanisms have scales for accurate adjustment, and here a mitre has been cut against the right hand fence.

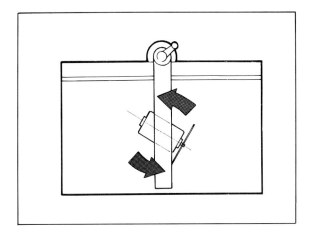

The motor rotates for in or out rip.

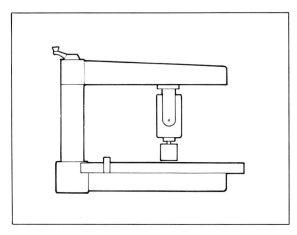

Radial arm saw set vertical with a sanding drum.

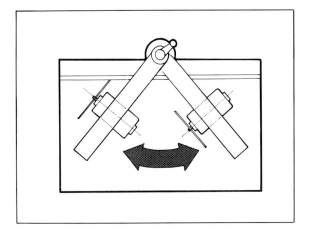

An angled crosscut with the arm swung radially.

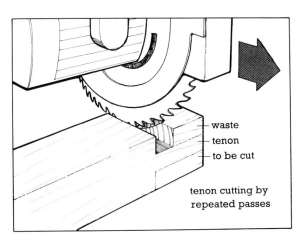

waste
tenon
to be cut

tenon cutting by
repeated passes

*A tenon formed by a series of overlapping cuts,
moving the wood along the fence after each pass.*

*Home-made wooden 'springs' fitted to a radial arm
sawtable. They are positioned to bend as a
workpiece is passed through; and hold it to the
fence.*

The wood should run smoothly along the fence
when being ripped, without problems. If, however, it either tends to jam against the fence or
try to move away from it, the blade is not parallel to the fence, and adjustment must be made
with reference to the handbook. Material which
is too thick to be ripped in one pass can be dealt
with in a similar manner to that employed when
crosscutting, a cut being made from each side.

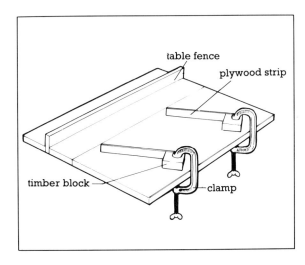

table fence

plywood strip

timber block

clamp

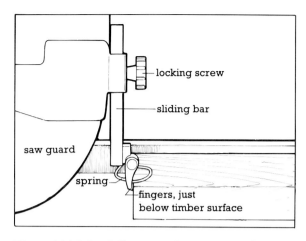

The anti-kick-back fingers and pressure spring are an important safety feature, and must be set carefully.

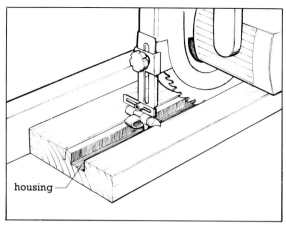

A housing cut with a sawblade, moving motor fractionally forward on arm after each cut.

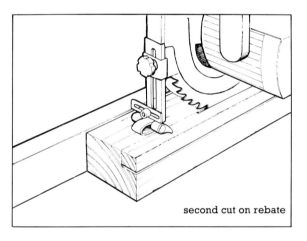

A rebate produced on a radial arm saw by two cuts to free a strip of waste. The second cut is made as shown here, ensuring maximum stability for the workpiece.

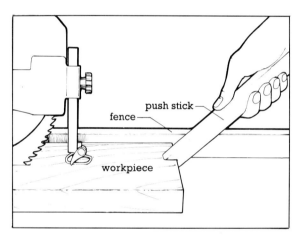

The correct ripping procedure, using push stick. Note that as the last few inches are cut, the anti-kick-back system is inoperative.

When ripping with the blade tilted, the anti-kick-back assembly can be fixed at a compensating angle.

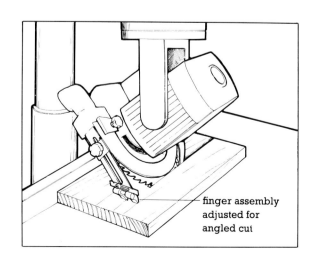

51

Anti-kick-back Fingers

The anti-kick-back fingers are small flat metal plates of a special shape, which are free to swing on the end of a vertical bar which can be adjusted in height. They are set to trail on the wood as it passes under the guard, and effectively prevent its being rejected by the blade and flung back at the sawyer. There is also a small shoe, made of spring steel, which should lightly touch the wood. This assembly is very efficient when correctly set, but the instructions in the saw handbook must be rigidly adhered to.

Riving Knives

A riving knife is essential when ripping timber with any circular saw, its function being to prevent the saw kerf from closing and pinching the back of the blade. If a blade other than that supplied with the saw is fitted, it is necessary to check that the riving knife can still do its job. On De Walt radials the riving knife is attached to the guard, by means of two screw knobs, and should be set so that its tip is just above the table, and its edge $\frac{1}{16}-\frac{1}{8}$ inch from the saw teeth.

Measuring the Cut

A rip scale is provided on the arm of the machine, and the distance of the blade from the fence can be set from it, although most workers prefer to use a rule for this job in the interests of accuracy, measuring from the fence to the tip of a tooth which is set inward, away from the front of the table. Note that all adjustments which involve the hands being near the blade must be carried out WITH THE PLUG REMOVED FROM THE SOCKET. It is NOT sufficient merely to switch the saw off.

Using a Push Stick

The importance of using push sticks cannot be overstressed. Fingers cannot normally be replaced, but the workshop is full of bits of wood. Although it is usually safe to begin a rip cut by hand, it should always be completed by applying pressure with a push stick, which is simply a piece of wood with a notch cut in it to fit over the workpiece. Bandsaw owners can produce fancy ones in a few minutes, and the edges can be rounded over on a sander to make the thing more comfortable to grip.

Bevel Ripping

Some users may have projects for which the process of bevel ripping will be very useful. In my case this is usually for the accurate production of staves to be built into multi-sided blanks for the turning of items such as tankards. There is nothing difficult about this, but the setting of the tilt of the motor must be done with great care, and the result checked on scrap wood. The handbook should be consulted for precise instructions as to the setting of the anti-kick-back assembly.

Resawing

Note that the process known as resawing, which can best be described as cutting a thick board in half edgewise, to produce two thinner ones, is not for beginners. It can be dangerous, requires the fitting of a special high fence to the machine, and is best avoided. This sort of work can be done with far less danger on a good bandsaw anyway.

Dust Protection

Ripping throws large quantities of sawdust back at the sawyer, and those who do not possess a good dust extractor will soon be rattling their piggy banks thoughtfully. In the absence of one of these marvellous pieces of equipment, however, it is best to wear a dust mask, and certainly to make sure that one's eyes are properly protected. Because of this problem, it is advisable to clean the motor tracks on the underside of the arm after a session of ripping. This is especially true when softwoods are involved, due to their resinous nature. No fluid or oil should be used, and the temptation to employ a solvent should be resisted. A dry rag will do the trick, but if this cleaning is neglected, the movement of the saw along the arm will rapidly become rough and unpleasant.

Sanding Attachments

The De Walt disc and drum sanders, which can be fitted on to the radial saw, are covered in the sander section, so there is no need for much detail here. In my view, however, these are both useful items, and I find the little drum sander invaluable for all sorts of jobs. Very little time is required to set up either sander for use, but a good dust extractor is a blessing if there is much abrasive work to be done. The drum sander is used unguarded, but the disc sander is meant to be used in conjunction with the ring guard.

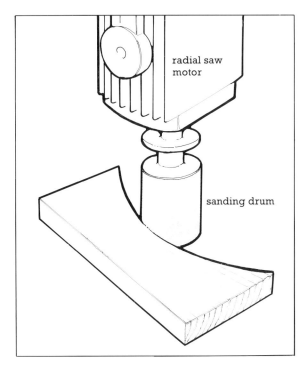

A radial arm saw with its motor tilted to vertical is ideal for driving a bobbin sander.

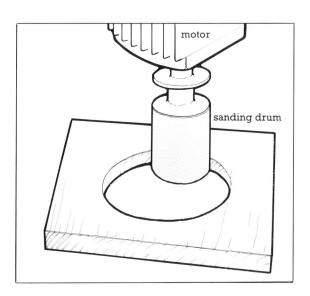

Bobbin sander used to clean up internal cut.

Router Attachments

Owners of Elu routers will find the router attachment bracket very interesting, and of great advantage for many routing operations. It holds the router firmly, and combines the versatility of the radial arm machine with the very high speed motor of the router. The motor of the radial arm is, of course, not used. The elevating handle is employed to position the router cutter at the desired height, and both the crosscut and

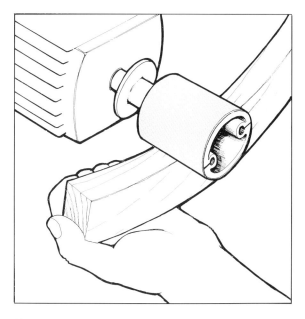

Freehand sanding of curved work on a bobbin sander.

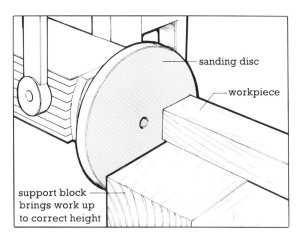

The De Walt radial arm machine in use with disc sander attachment. Note the use of a wood block as a sanding table, to position work against disc.

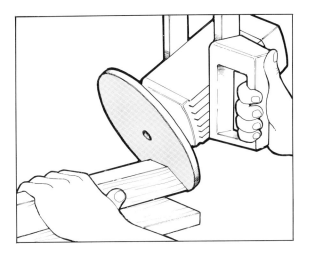

Angle sanding with De Walt radial. The work is stationary, the disc is moved backward and forward.

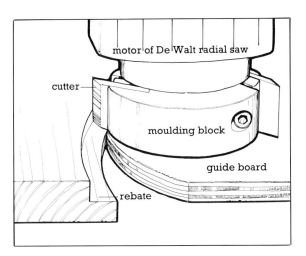

Rebating a curved edge by running the workpiece against a curved board fixed to the sawtable. The De Walt motor is tilted to vertical, and there is no danger of over cutting.

rip facilities of the radial can be exploited to good effect. This system is particularly useful for routing out areas of a job, the rotating cutter being lowered into the wood, and the workpiece moved around on the table. Further details of this kind of work will be found in the router section.

Sabre Saw Attachments

The sabre saw attachment is really a jigsaw, but it operates upside down by comparison with normal jigsaws, just as hand planers work in an inverted position as compared with planer/thicknessers. This being so, the teeth of the blades supplied for this attachment have to point down rather than up as is normally the case, so that the cutting action holds the workpiece down on the table rather than lifting it. The correct blades must therefore be fitted to this device at all times.

It is necessary for the end of the blade to pass below the table surface, so a hole must be drilled to permit this. Once the attachment has been fitted, it can be positioned over the hole, and lowered as required by the elevating handle of the machine. It is then switched on, and the wood is fed to it. A saw of this kind has less depth of cut than a bandsaw, but it has one

advantage, which is its ability to cut internal shapes. A hole is drilled in the waste part of the workpiece to allow access for the blade, and straight or curved cuts can be made with ease. It is perhaps not worth setting up one of these tools for very small amounts of work, but where a quantity of jigsawing is involved it is well worth having one.

Drilling Attachments

A small drill chuck can be obtained, which screws onto the motor shaft, and there is of course plenty of power available for drilling purposes. It is also true to say that the versatility of the radial arm machine enhances the virtues of drilling in this way, but this accessory is likely to appeal mainly to those who have no alternative form of drilling equipment. A sharp spade bit (otherwise known as a flat bit) will work very well, however, and the cost of these chucks is not great.

In conclusion, if machines of this kind are well designed and engineered, they will be accurate, and will represent a sound investment. If they are poorly designed and badly constructed, they will be inaccurate, and may well be dangerous.

6
BANDSAWS

Bandsaws are fascinating machines, but only the really good ones are worth buying for serious woodwork. A good bandsaw, with a good blade fitted and all adjustments and settings correct, is a delight to use, and is capable of performing a wide range of woodworking operations satisfactorily. Poorly engineered versions are nothing but a nuisance, and can drive the unfortunate user to the verge of hysteria. They will also cause considerable expense in that they break blades frequently, and bandsaw blades are not cheap.

Construction

In essence a bandsaw is a metal box of peculiar shape, containing either two or three wheels, which normally have rubber 'tyres' on which the blade runs. One wheel is driven by a motor positioned outside the box or case, and one can be moved by means of an adjuster, to enable tension to be applied to the blade. Some bandsaws have more than one speed, but this is not necessary for purely woodworking applications.

The bandsaw casing is made in a shape which permits the fitting of a table, which may or may not be capable of being tilted from the horizontal for angle cutting. There are, therefore, two main sections to a bandsaw case, these being connected by a relatively narrow vertical piece known as the column. In poorly made bandsaws weakness of the column permits flexing of the case under load, which prohibits accurate cutting, and in extreme cases frequently causes the blade to slip off the wheels.

MiniMax bandsaw, with both covers removed. Construction is very robust, and the heavy, finely balanced wheels, help to give very efficient results.

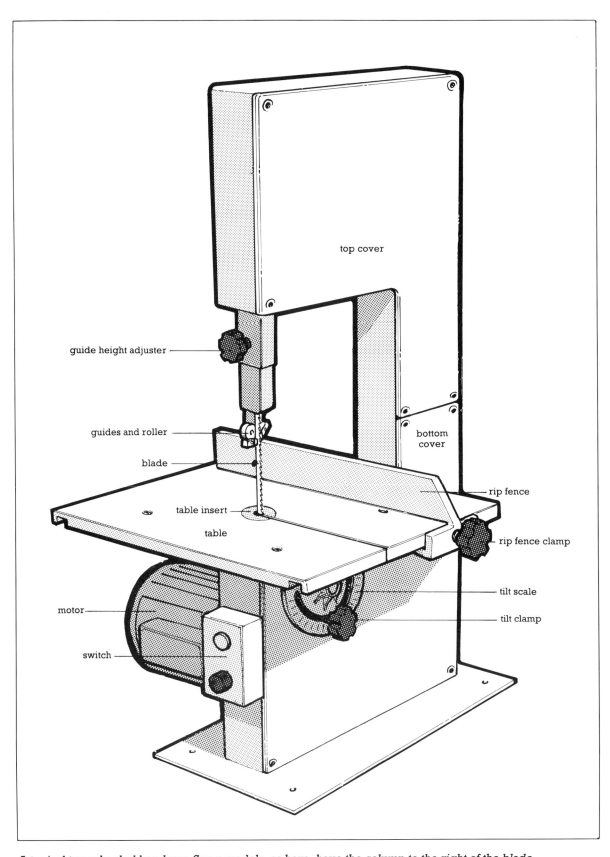

top cover

guide height adjuster

bottom cover

guides and roller

blade

rip fence

table insert

table

rip fence clamp

tilt scale

motor

tilt clamp

switch

A typical two wheeled bandsaw. Some models, as here, have the column to the right of the blade.

The distance between the blade and the column is known as the throat, and three-wheeled bandsaws are sometimes selected by beginners simply because this distance is greater on three wheeled versions. It is not always realised that only the waste passes through the throat, and in practice the two-wheeled machine is preferable because its wheels are larger. Small bandsaw wheels quickly induce metal fatigue in the blade, which causes cracking and early blade failure. For this reason the heavier gauge blued steel blades, which are by far the best, cannot be used on small three-wheelers.

On many bandsaws a circular insert is provided to fit into a hole in the table where the blade passes through, and removal of this will facilitate inspection of the lower thrust bearing and guide assembly. There will also be a slit in the table from the front edge to the insert hole, through which the blade will be passed when being removed or fitted. Table tilt is provided by means of trunnions under the table, and an adjustable stop is fitted so that the table can be returned to its normal position at ninety degrees to the blade without the need for any check.

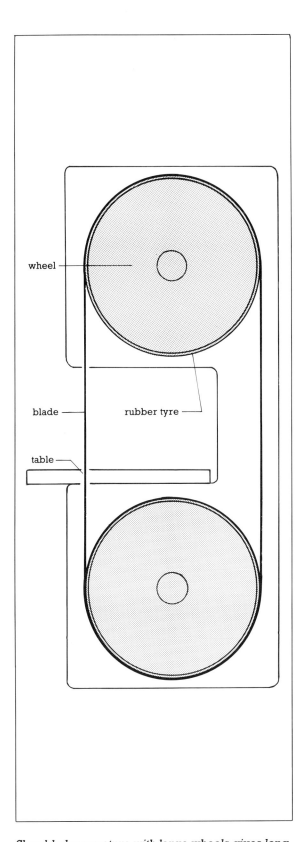

Slow blade curvature with large wheels gives long blade life with blued steel blades.

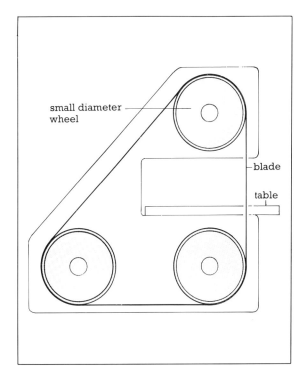

Three wheeled bandsaws have small wheels, and are in general less efficient than the two wheeled versions.

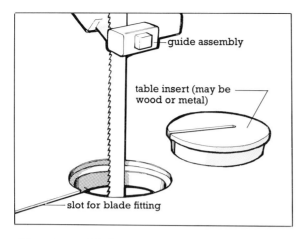

A bandsaw table insert.

Depth of Cut

The most important factor with bandsaws for most users is the depth of cut, which on a good machine is the thickness of timber which can pass under the upper guide assembly at the maximum height setting. On poor machines there may be plenty of room under the guides, but the chances of successful cutting on thick timber are slim.

Depth of cut on an average home user bandsaw is around 6 inches, although there are larger and more expensive models which will give up to 11 inches. These big machines require one and a half to two horsepower, the smaller ones

are usually fitted with three quarter to one horsepower units. An underpowered bandsaw is extremely frustrating when used for cutting thick hardwoods, and it is wise to go for a machine with power to spare.

Rip Fences

Before discussing the provisions incorporated for controlling the blade, it may be as well to look at two facilities which are available for machines of this type: the rip fence and the mitre guide. Few bandsaws will perform well with either of these items, though there are some exceptions. In general terms, the circular saw is the precision straight line cutter, and the bandsaw is at its best when following a marked line to produce curved shapes.

The rip fence is a straight bar of metal which clamps to the front of the table, and can be set at a chosen distance from the blade. Its purpose is to guide timber which is being cut through along its length, the process being known as ripping or ripsawing. In many cases the results will be disappointing, because the blade will wander, but machines like the Mini-Max, shown in the photographs, perform well.

Mitre Guides

Bandsaw mitre guides usually run in a slot which is machined into the table in a fore and aft direction, because they have to move with the wood as the cut is made. They are intended to facilitate ninety degree crosscuts, or crosscuts

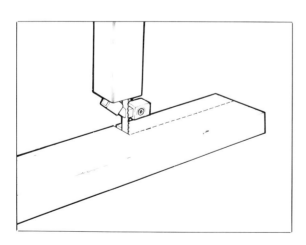

Where a short and a long cut are required to meet, the short one is made first, since the blade can easily be backed out.

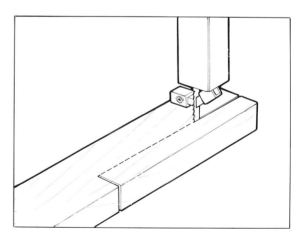

When the second (long) cut is made, the waste falls away.

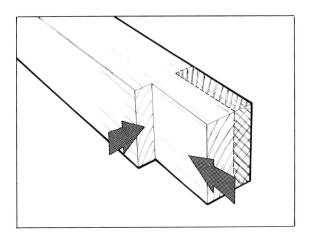

Tenon cutting is simple with a good bandsaw. Stop blocks can be used to limit the cuts.

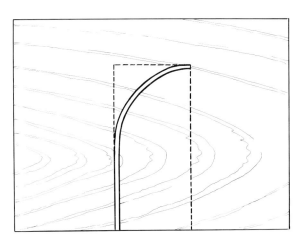

Removing a narrow rectangle of waste can be done as shown.

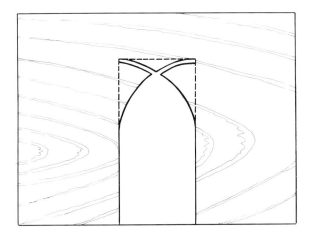

The first two cuts are swung across to the opposite corners, the waste pieces at the sides are

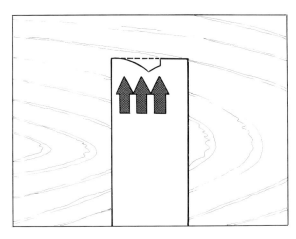

removed, and the remaining waste is 'nibbled' away by the blade.

made at an angle between zero and ninety degrees, this being selected by means of a scale. Mitre guides for bandsaws are frequently optional extras, and in most cases they are not worth buying.

Thrust Bearings

However good a bandsaw blade may be, its efficiency will depend to a large extent upon the quality and accurate setting of the thrust bearings, blade guides, track adjuster, and to some extent the tension adjuster.

Thrust bearings, or in some cases thrust rollers, appear in various guises on different types of machine, but their function is always the same. They prevent the blade from being pushed backwards, and so dislodged from the wheels as the wood is cut. They are positioned behind the blade, and can be adjusted fore and aft. When correctly set they should almost, but not quite, touch the back of the blade when the machine is not cutting.

Blade Guides

Blade guides are very important, and too often neglected. They are designed to prevent the blade from twisting, and so deviating from its intended path. The material from which these guides are made may be metal, plastic, or

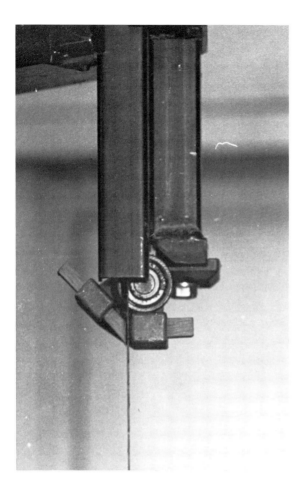

The blade guard carries the upper guide and thrust roller assembly, and can be adjusted up or down relative to the table. In use the guides must be set as close as possible to the work.

Correct setting of guard for maximum safety and blade support is shown here. Note also the front trunnion, which permits the tilting of the table. There is an identical trunnion at the rear.

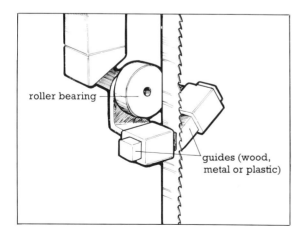

A typical guide and support bearing unit for a bandsaw.

hardwood. They are fitted in pairs, so that they present flat surfaces to the sides of the blade, with which they should not make contact when the machine is at rest or not actually cutting. The combination of track adjustment and guide setting should be such that the teeth of the blade cannot pass between the faces of the guides at any time.

Track Adjusters

The track adjuster is a control at the back of the bandsaw casing, which when turned causes the upper wheel to tilt forward or backward. This control is often designed to be adjusted by means of an Allen key or a spanner, rather than a hand controller, to avoid interference by those who cannot resist turning knobs. Good bandsaws will remain accurately on their set track, which means that the position of the blade on the wheels will not change. Bad machines will not behave in this manner, and are therefore a constant source of aggravation, since it will readily be appreciated that any deviation from the set tracking position will move the blade relative to the guides and thrust bearings. Track adjusters are sometimes provided with a locking nut as an added safeguard against unintentional alteration to the setting, but these should not be tightened too much, and when they have been tightened the setting should be checked again to ensure that it has not altered.

Note that the approved manner of setting track on a bandsaw is to remove the plug from the wall socket, take off the front covers, and set the track while turning the wheels in the normal direction of rotation by hand. NEVER run a bandsaw with the covers off, this being a very dangerous practice.

Setting the Tension

Tension on bandsaw blades is a worry to many new owners, because there are no simple rules for setting it. Tension is applied before the track is set, and is a matter of getting used to the machine. Some makers suggest approaches to the problem, but they are never a complete answer, and the subject is controversial. I feel that if a beginner applies just a little more tension than seems right, the result will be reasonably satisfactory, and experience with a particular machine is the real answer.

Vibration

When selecting a bandsaw, try to find one which has heavy steel wheels, which have been accurately balanced to eliminate vibration. These machines need the stored energy which is provided by wheels of this type, in rather the same way as a car engine needs its flywheel. This factor helps to prevent blade snatch, which is a common cause of breakage. In my experience the longer a bandsaw takes to come to rest when switched off, the better it is likely to perform, and one soon acquires the habit of dropping the guard down to the table. Some of the bigger bandsaws are fitted with brakes in the interests of safety.

Choosing your Blade

It is extremely important for a new owner of a bandsaw to have a full understanding of the types of blade available, and to use good blades which will run true, and allow the machine to give its best. There are two distinct types of blade, one of which is silver in colour, the other dark blue. Silver blades are relatively low in price, but their performance reflects the fact. They are of thinner gauge metal than the blued steel variety, and so are suitable for machines with small wheels, which unfortunately cannot cope with the heavier type. They lose their sharpness rapidly, break quite frequently, and their performance is unpredictable. In many cases the machine is blamed for this abysmal performance, which is unfortunate.

Some confusion is to be expected in the early stages of using a machine which has a high degree of versatility, and the wide range of blades which can be purchased for bandsaws is at the root of some of the problems. The essence of this is that blades or blade material can be obtained in various widths, and with a variety of tooth patterns. This is all very well, but whereas it is normally a quick and simple matter to change the blade on a circular saw, the process is a complicated one with a bandsaw, and can take a beginner up to twenty minutes. The result is that most people end up with a favourite width and tooth pattern, which they use for almost all their cutting. The width of a blade limits the minimum radius which it can be expected to cut efficiently, while the tooth pattern affects the speed of the cutting and the smoothness or otherwise of the sawn surface.

Close up of upper bandsaw wheel, showing the holes which have been drilled during manufacture to balance the wheel exactly.

For practical purposes in the home workshop it is not necessary to become deeply involved in bandsaw blade theory. In simple terms the important facts are as follows. Blades are described in terms of TPI or PPI, these meaning teeth per inch or points per inch. One refers to the number of complete teeth in one inch of blade, the other to the number of tooth points. For most of us this is academic, and has no practical significance other than in the case of blades which have very few teeth. The beginner is likely to be concerned with maximum quality of finish on the sawn surface, or with rapid cutting of thick timbers, and in some cases with a compromise between the two.

Blades with a relatively large number of small teeth can produce a better finish, but they cut more slowly, and are not very efficient in terms of clearing the waste from the gullets of the blade (the gaps between the teeth) especially if the wood is damp. Blades with fewer but larger teeth cut faster and clear their gullets better, but usually give a lower quality of surface finish. The blade which is most efficient in terms of gullet clearance is the 'skip tooth', which has very wide gullets because every other tooth is missing. My own choice for about ninety per cent of my bandsaw work is a $\frac{3}{8}$ inch wide skip tooth with three teeth per inch. Good quality blade of this type does in fact produce a reasonable sawn finish, but most of my work goes into a lathe, is subsequently sanded, is trimmed on a router to exact size with the aid of a template, or is passed over a planer. Students attending courses in my workshop frequently express surprise at the finish produced by a blue blade of this pattern, and at the speed of cutting.

Set of the Blade

Blued steel blade is manufactured as strip metal, the teeth are then cut, the set is applied to them, and the teeth are hardened leaving the rest of the blade soft to reduce the effects of metal fatigue. Set is the slight outward inclination of the teeth of a sawblade, with each alternate tooth leaning the opposite way to those adjacent to it, as described in the circular saw chapter. Set is particularly vital to bandsaw blades, since it provides a kerf (width of cut) which is wider than the thickness of the blade, and so permits the blade to swing in the kerf when cutting curves. With silver blades the set tends to disappear fairly quickly if the blade runs fully on the wheels, because the teeth which bend towards the wheel are bent back.

This results in a problem known as lead, the blade wandering from its intended path in the direction of maximum set. For this reason machines which are fitted with these blades generally have in their instruction leaflet the warning

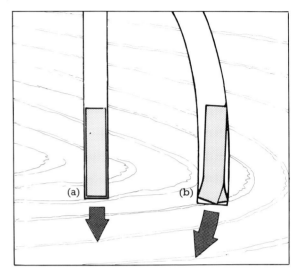

(a) Blade with inadequate set cannot swing in the kerf to follow a curve.
(b) Adequate set gives wider kerf, so blade can swing.

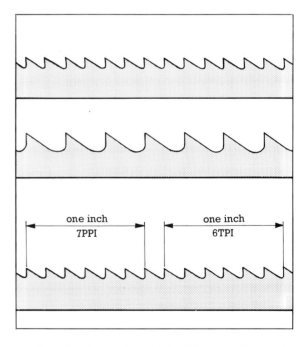

Bandsaw blades can be obtained in many different patterns, with coarse or fine teeth. The bottom sketch shows how blades can be described in terms of teeth per inch (TPI) or points per inch (PPI).

that the blade should run with its teeth over-hanging the front edges of the wheels, not to protect the rubber tyres, but to safeguard the set. In practice however this is a bad idea, since it is very difficult to keep narrow blades on the wheels if they are tracked in this manner, and blued steel blades can be run fully on the tyres without any problem.

Making your Own Blade

A further point, which applies only to the blue blades, is that many people, myself included, make up their own blades from large bulk rolls of blade material. This makes the blades a great deal cheaper, and permits the rapid repair of a blade should it break prematurely. It is also an unfortunate fact that ready made blades fre-quently break at the joint when they have done very little work.

The process of making up a blade is quite simple, and well within the capabilities of most home woodworkers, but it is greatly facilitated by the purchase of a jig which will align the blade correctly and clamp it in place while the joint is made. The more ingenious worker will probably make up a jig in the workshop for this purpose. (See p. 33).

DO NOT under any circumstances open the package or container in which the bulk blade is supplied, or there may well be an accident as the contents fly out. A short length of blade will be found projecting from the package, and one merely pulls sufficient blade out, and cuts it off with a pair of tin snips, cutting in the centre of one of the gaps between the teeth. The next step is to grind the ends of the blade gently at an approximate forty five degree angle, to pro-duce what is known as a scarfed joint. This pro-vides more bonding area than a straight butt joint, but the freshly ground areas must not be touched with the fingers.

Three items, apart from a jig and a length of blade, are required for the making of a blade: a butane torch, some silver solder, and some suitable flux. These can be obtained from good tool stores, and after a little practice on short lengths cut from the bulk stock of blade, the procedure will be found to be quite simple. The ground ends are first tinned, which means that they are heated to a cherry red and coated with solder, some flux having first been applied. When the tinning has been completed, the blade is placed in the jig with the ground ends

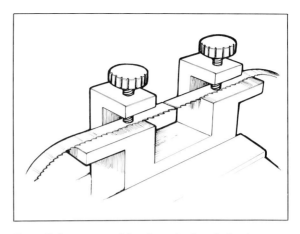

A small jig, mounted in a bench vice, helps in silver soldering blued steel blades for bandsaws.

overlapping correctly, and is clamped in po-sition. These jigs are quite small, and can be held in a vice. The torch flame is now applied until the solder is seen to flow, whereupon the joint is grasped in a pair of pliers, and the flame is removed. Any excess solder should be re-moved with a file, and the blade is ready for fitting.

Safety Points

Bandsaws are certainly less dangerous than cir-cular saws, but they can inflict serious injury if proper attention is not paid to safety. Most of the blade is covered by the casing, but it is obvious that sufficient must be left exposed for any spec-ific cut. Leaving too much blade exposed is a common cause of accidents, so the guard must always be adjusted so that it is just above the upper surface of the material, and since the upper guide assembly is attached to the guard, this also means that it is as close as possible to the lower guides, and can do its job efficiently.

Danger is always present when timber is ma-chined with inadequate support, and in this the bandsaw is no exception. If the surface of the wood which is to be placed on the table is not flat, it should be made so by planing or belt sanding before the job commences. Round stock, such as dowel, presents obvious prob-lems, which are best overcome by making a V block to give satisfactory support. A V block is simply a piece of wood in which two angled cuts have been made, so removing a V shaped sec-tion. If the round material is to be crosscut, the block is placed against the mitre fence, if the

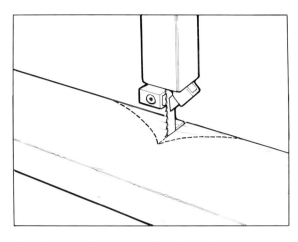

Avoiding bandsaw traps. Cut through waste to centre, so that waste wood can fall away when dotted lines are followed.

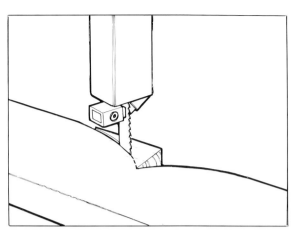

Once the preliminary cut has been made, the small detail can be dealt with very easily.

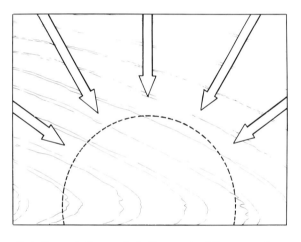

Cuts through the waste to the marked line permit the waste to fall away as the shape is cut.

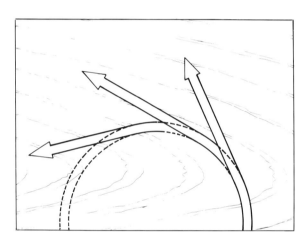

When a bandsaw blade is too wide for a required radius, a series of tangential cuts can be made.

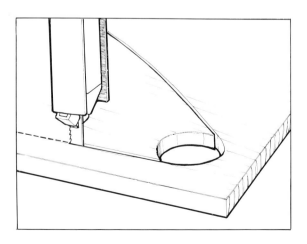

A few holes drilled at strategic points can greatly ease the problems for the bandsawyer.

wood is to be ripped the V block is fed forwards endwise into the moving blade for a short distance, then clamped firmly to the table. The wood is then placed in the V and the sawing can be done safely. Note that in all ripping operations the hands must be kept clear of the blade, so the last few inches of such cuts are performed either by placing one hand behind the blade and pulling the wood, or by means of a push stick.

The cutting of branch wood is potentially dangerous, and should be avoided by beginners, though this sort of cutting is a frequent requirement for woodturners. The problem is that wood which is uneven may move suddenly while it is being cut. This may merely jam the blade in the wood, usually kinking it badly and rendering it unfit for further work, or in extreme cases could pull the worker's fingers into contact with the blade. Those who cut branch wood take care to ensure that there is full contact between wood and table at the point where the cut takes place.

In more orthodox bandsawing operations there is less danger, but there are traps for the unwary, and it is easy to arrive at a point where the cut cannot be continued, and it is difficult to retreat. The illustrations will clarify this, but one thing which must be kept in mind is that backing out of a cut on these machines is bad practice. The blade, as I explained earlier, is prevented from being pushed off the wheels when cutting, by the thrust bearings. It can, however, come off the wheels quite easily if the wood is pulled backwards, and this must be avoided as far as possible. The answer is to plan the cutting, which becomes second nature after some experience has been gained, and the illustrations will explain this quite clearly.

Cutting a Tenon

Good bandsaws can be used for the cutting of tenons (see mortisers p. 82) and in skilled hands, a machine which cuts accurately will produce good work. The cutting of a tenon requires the making of two short cuts and two longer ones, which meet and so remove sections of timber. This is a good example of the fact that where a short cut is to meet a longer one to remove a piece of waste, the short cut is made first, so that it is not necessary to back out of the longer one.

Compound Bandsawing

Compound bandsawing is a useful technique in some forms of woodwork, and is commonly employed by carvers as a means of removing waste from a blank to leave a rough approximation of the required shape. The first job is to draw the front and side elevations of the project on adjacent sides of the block, and if the work is of a repetitive nature it is customary to make templates from plywood or hardboard to facilitate this. When the cutting has been done to the marking on one side of the wood, the waste pieces are replaced, and held in position by adhesive tape or glue. The second marked side is then attended to, and the result is eventually carved.

Bandsaws are extremely versatile, and although those who have never used one often wonder what use it would be to them, they are likely, after a few months of using one, to wonder how they ever managed without it.

Good bandsaws are very effective as tenon cutting machines, as shown here. This sort of work calls for high quality blades, of the blued steel variety, and tenons can be cut with surprising speed and accuracy.

7
JIGSAWS

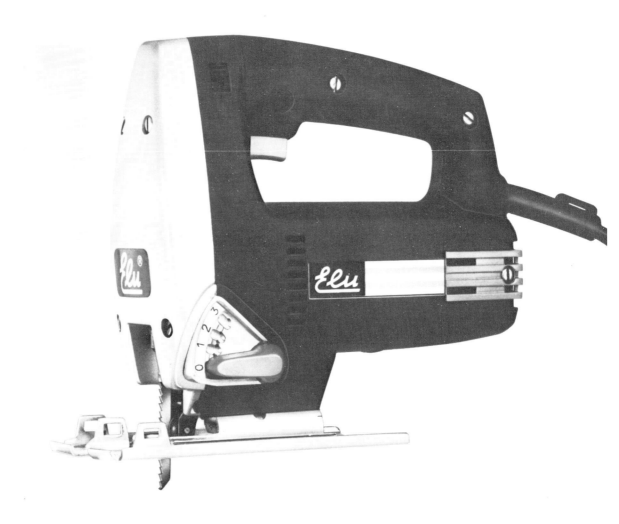

A typical jigsaw with tilting sole plate for angle cutting.

The portable jigsaw – known in America as a sabre saw – is essentially a shape cutting tool, and is very good at cutting curves. This is very much the province of the bandsaw, but the jigsaw is portable and can be taken to the work. Its cutting action is reciprocal, and it cuts only on the upward stroke, and is therefore not particularly fast in action. The maximum depth of cut obtainable is about two inches, but it is nevertheless very handy for lots of jobs on work within its capacity. It does have one important advantage over the bandsaw, in that it can be used for internal cuts if a hole is first drilled in the waste area to permit the insertion of the blade.

Most jigsaws now have some form of variable speed control, which is mainly intended to permit them to be used for the cutting of metal, plastics, and other materials if the appropriate blade is fitted. This may not matter too much to many woodworkers, but there is another system now quite commonly employed on these tools, which provides what is known as an orbital action for the blade, the degree of orbital action being adjustable. This can be very useful, because it offers a means of cutting slowly where a fine finish is needed on the sawn edge, with minimum setting, or of cutting very fast where the sawn edge is not an important consideration.

The root of all this is that a jigsaw blade moves up and down in the cut, and has some difficulty in emptying its gullets, unlike the blade of a bandsaw, the teeth of which, having cut, emerge from the wood and have ample time for chip clearance on their journey around the wheels. The orbital action allows the jigsaw blade to 'back off' after each upward cutting stroke, the amount of movement being determined by the setting of the control.

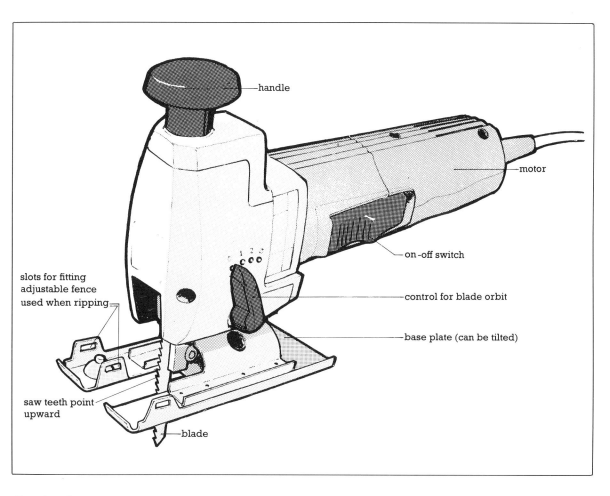

A typical jigsaw.

Construction

The jigsaw is a simple enough machine, consisting of an electric motor in a casing with a handle fitted, in which are located the switch trigger, and the locking button which enables the motor to be kept running without the trigger being held. The motor imparts the desired reciprocal motion to a shaft in which the blade is fitted, and a sole plate is provided to support the machine on the surface of the workpiece. The sole plate is usually capable of being tilted for angle cutting, and a scale is attached.

The normal approach to following marked lines was always to twist the tool about as required, but some models now have a knob at the top of the casing which can be used to rotate the blade. Some workers swear by this idea, but others swear at it.

Backtracking

Jigsaws can be backtracked in the cut quite easily, there being no chance of pulling the blade off the machine, as is the case with bandsaws, and this is a helpful feature. It will be noted that there is no possibility of getting stuck in a cut through lack of planning, because the machine can be switched off and withdrawn from the wood.

Safety Points

Any power driven cutting tool can cause injury if wrongly or carelessly handled, and although jigsaws are not high on my list of tools to beware

of, accidents do happen, so the same methodical and careful approach should be employed with these tools as with any other.

One fact which will be revealed by a study of the illustrations is that in most cutting operations part of the blade protrudes through the bottom surface of the wood, and on thin work this will be by an appreciable amount. This part of the blade is unguarded, because there is no way of guarding it, and it is all too easily forgotten. People have lost fingers by placing them under the wood, having forgotten the blade projection, and the answer is of course to adopt from the very first day the habit of never putting any fingers under the workpiece.

This blade projection under the work also means that material being cut must be supported in a manner which permits the blade to move around without striking the bench, or anything which may be lying on its surface. The whereabouts of the electrical cable should also be considered, since it is quite easy in some cases to have a loop of this under the work.

Cutting with a Jigsaw

The actual process of cutting with a jigsaw does not require much explanation, the following of a marked line becomes quite easy after a little practice on scrap wood, but the workpiece should be securely clamped whenever possible. Most lines in jigsaw work are followed by cutting just outside the marks, being careful not to touch them. This means that the finished piece is slightly oversize, but it can then be

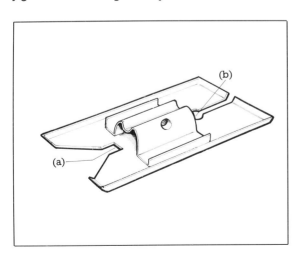

Reversible sole plate for a jigsaw. Used with the blade at (a) for general work, or at (b) to give full support on thin wood.

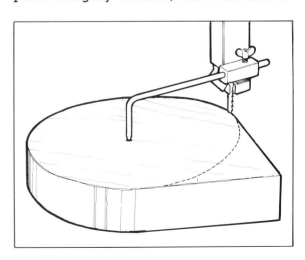

Circle cutting on a bandsaw. Various forms of jig can be used, but most professionals cut by eye to a marked line.

sanded or template-routed to the finished dimensions.

It is possible to use fences for ripping, and these are standard equipment. Jigsaws do not respond to this approach as well as some tools, the blade tending to wander in the grain, but a lot will depend upon the quality of the tool, and in particular of its blade.

Newcomers to these tools often find that they are continually breaking blades, but unless a very poor type of blade is in use, this is normally due to lack of skill on the part of the operator, and the problem fades with time. Any powered cutting tool should be allowed to cut, not forced to do so, and attempting to cut round a radius which is too tight for the width of the blade is a common error.

Other jigsaw applications will be found to require the same sort of treatment as bandsaw work, and the chapter dealing with bandsaws should provide all that is needed in the way of information. The use of these tools is very much a matter of common sense.

Blades

Top quality jigsaws usually have top quality blades, which means that they are not initially cheap. They do, however, last a very long time, and they perform extremely well. The high quality of these machines and of the blades supplied for it enable rip fences to be used effectively, and even permit the accurate cutting of circles by means of a trammel arm, which is an accessory available from the makers. Trammel arms are discussed in the router section, so I will not repeat the description here, but they are inexpensive, and with a little ingenuity it is possible to produce home-made versions which work well.

There is no need to worry too much about the range of blades offered by specific makers, since the majority of these are intended for cutting materials other than wood, but there are one or two points worth mentioning. One of these concerns safety, both as regards the user and in respect of the workpiece. This is that jigsaws should always be switched off and allowed to stop before being withdrawn from a cut. If this is not observed the rapidly moving blade may strike the upper surface of the wood as it is withdrawn, which might cause an accident, and would certainly damage the workpiece.

Another point is that some jigsaw blades have a special tooth at the tip, which enables the blade to peck its way through a piece of wood, so avoiding the process of drilling a starting hole. This should, in my view, not be attempted by anyone not used to jigsaws, although it is not really difficult after sufficient practice on scrap softwood. The procedure is to place the tips of the toes of the sole plate firmly on the wood with the saw tilted forward so that the blade is clear of the work surface. The machine is then switched on, and firm contact between sole plate toes and wood is maintained as the saw is slowly tilted back until the sole plate is flat on the wood. This can obviously be very useful, but I would consider it to be suitable for experienced jigsaw users only.

In a bandsaw, every tooth takes its share of the workload in turn, but this is rarely so with jigsaws unless they are constantly used on thick wood. Toymakers use them a great deal, and those who use plywood for various purposes, but it is a pity that when they are blunt there are still quite a few teeth which are as good as new, since only those near the sole plate have been cutting. I am advised that those of a frugal nature sometimes break off the upper part of the blade, which has become blunt, and grind the remainder to fit the machine. There is then less potential depth of cut, but still sufficient for what they have to do. I never have time to fiddle about with ideas like this because woodworking is for me a means of survival, but there may be merit in the suggestion.

Jigsaws are good fun, and I suggest the initial purchase of some fine toothed blades for thin wood, and some fairly coarse ones for rough cutting. Keep the sole plate flat on the wood during all cuts, and the use of this tool will soon become instinctive.

8

PLANERS

Next in importance to a sawbench or a radial arm saw is a planer of some kind, and careful consideration must be given to the purchase of such tools, or money may be wasted. There is great joy in using a sharp and correctly set hand plane, and I often miss the beautiful curly shavings which surrounded me when I was young, but hand planing is hard work and time-consuming when there is a lot of it to be done. A good planer, kept in adjustment, with sharp knives, does an excellent job, and there is a pleasure of a different kind to be found in using these machines.

In this chapter I will discuss three types of planer which are in common use, these being the small surface planer, known in America as a jointer; the planer thicknesser, which is considerably more expensive; and the hand held portable electric planer.

SURFACE PLANERS

Planers are usually referred to by the length of their knives, so a ten inch planer is a machine which will plane wood up to ten inches in width. Surface planers are usually quite small, having knives from four to six inches long, but they are relatively inexpensive, and can be very useful. The first planer I ever owned was of this type, and in fact was an attachment for a Coronet Major universal woodworking machine. Its knives were four and a half inches long, so it was rather limited in its applications, but it did its job well, and it had the ability to cut rebates quickly and accurately, which I found invaluable.

Construction

The heart of a planer is its cutter block, a heavy steel cylinder which is accurately balanced, and rotates in high quality bearings. Two, or sometimes three, slots are cut lengthwise in the block, to permit the insertion of the knives, and provision is usually made for adjustment of their projection. In front of the cutter block, relative to the operator, is a flat table known as the feed table, or sometimes the front table, and a take off table of equal proportions is fitted behind the block. The height of each table can be altered by turning an adjusting screw, although some cheap machines have fixed take off tables. The cutter block is driven by belt and pulleys, the motor being positioned in a convenient place. The tables and cutter block are attached to the body of the planer, and the machine is often quite heavy. Steel tables are preferred by most workers, but I have found cast alloy ones to be quite satisfactory if they have been well made.

In theory a three-bladed planer will give a better finish to the wood than one with two blades, but this is true only if all three knives have equal projection from the block, which in practice is difficult to achieve, and most home workshop planers are two-bladed.

Safety Points

Planers are fitted with fences against which the wood rides when being machined, and which can often be tilted for planing angled edges. There are also guards, which must be used at all times, otherwise a nasty accident is simply waiting to happen. Familiarity must never be allowed to breed contempt with machinery, and certainly not with planers, which are capable of inflicting severe injuries.

Assembly of the Machine

When a new machine is received, the first stage is to check it over thoroughly. It may have been in perfect order when it left the factory, or maybe it was not, but in either case it should not be started until it has been checked. A few knocks in transit can easily throw things out of adjustment. The instructions which follow, together with those provided by the makers, will enable you to set up a planer correctly, and when this job has been done a few times it will become almost second nature. It must always be borne in mind, however, that machines can only be as accurate as the person who sets them up.

Setting the Knives

The setting of the knives in the cutter block is critical, and should never be hurried. The knives are available in three different materials, and it helps to fit the right type for the kind of work in progress. Knives fitted as standard by the makers are of chrome steel, which works very well on softwoods and most hardwoods. Where long runs on difficult or abrasive timbers are required, blades made of high speed steel are preferable. This steel contains cobalt, and is much harder than the standard blades, but it is still possible for the user to hone the edges with an oilstone when they become dull. The ultimate, for use when processing man made board, or planing nasty mineral impregnated timbers such as keruing, is tungsten carbide, which is very hard indeed. Knives tipped with this will last a very long time between grindings, but this operation can only be done on special machines, so the knives must be sent away to be ground. Blades of this kind are extremely expensive.

Some planers, in the cheaper range, have no system built in to assist in the knife setting process, and they can be quite fiddly. The standard answer to this is to use a large magnet laid on the take off table, and let the knives 'hang' from this as they are tightened in the block. The idea is to achieve equal projection from the block along the full length of each knife. Better machines, like the De Walt, do have systems which vastly simplify this, being fitted with small grub screws in the block which will raise or lower the knives when they are turned.

As is the case with all adjustments to machines, the plug must first be removed from the wall socket. The guard and fence are then removed, and each knife is dealt with in turn. Rather than merely slackening the clamping screws and adjusting, it is a good idea to remove each knife completely from the block, and thoroughly clean both knife and slot using a small brush and some solvent. These areas are then dried with a soft cloth, and a thin coating of machine oil is applied. The precise method of setting up the knives does tend to vary very slightly among users, but I will describe here the method which I have used successfully for many years.

I have stated that the knives should be level with the take off table, but in practice many people, myself included, run with them fractionally high. This must only be by a whisker, or it will do more harm than good. Incorrect knife setting produces phenomena which puzzle and frustrate beginners, who tend to blame the machine. If the knives are set a little too high, a slightly deeper cut will be produced as the last inch or so of the wood passes over them. Only one knife may perhaps be high, but the result will be the same. If, on the other hand, the setting of the knives has erred on the low side, the workpiece will catch against the edge of the take off table. It is possible to hitch it over and continue with the cut, but if this is done a slow taper will be produced on the material. If this is unobserved, and planing continues, the taper will become quite evident. The necessary ad-

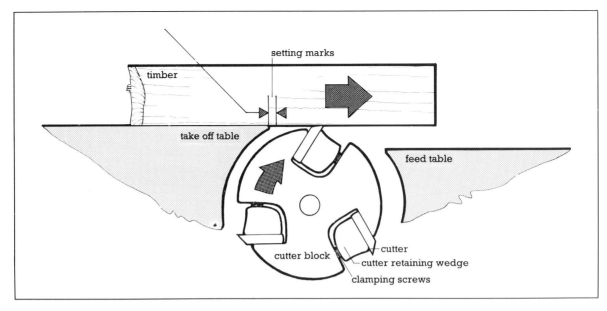

A piece of planed timber is used to check the setting of the knives. Each knife should move the wood forward as the block is rotated slowly by hand, about ⅛ inch, as shown by the pencil marks.

justment in such cases may be minute, but it must be made.

The edges of the knives must also be parallel to the surface of the take off table, which they will be if the following procedure is adhered to. The first step is to release the clamping screws from one blade, and take it out of the block for cleaning. If screw adjusters are fitted they will have to wind the knives fully up before they can be removed. After cleaning, the knife is refitted and wound down to its approximate original position. A simple aid to fitting is now employed, this being a piece of wood with a perfectly straight edge, having two pencil marks at the edge of one face spaced a fraction under one eighth of an inch apart. Precise adjustment is achieved by placing this wood on the take off table on edge, so that the marks can be seen, and adjusting the knives so that when rotated by hand they move the wood forward by the exact spacing of the marks. They should be checked at intervals along their length, then tightened securely and checked again. Each knife receives this treatment, and if the job has been done properly the machine is ready for use.

Surface Planing

The actual operation of surface planing a piece of wood is quite simple if the knives are correctly set, but fine cuts do produce the best finishes, as is the case with a hand plane, and about a sixteenth of an inch is enough to remove at one pass. Heavy cuts may tear the surface, and could produce a kick back, especially when blunt knives are in use. The planer guard may seem to be a bit of a nuisance initially, but it must be in place, and one soon becomes used to it. Note also that planers up to about twelve inches wide are now used in home workshops, although most of the wood planed will be much narrower. It is therefore good policy to distribute the wear on the blades evenly, by moving the fence and guard occasionally.

Taking as an example a square piece of wood which is to be planed on all sides, or a piece which is not quite square and is to be made so on the planer, the first step is to plane one side, cutting with the grain of the wood where possible. A pass on the planer is made by placing the wood on the feed table and in contact with the fence. It is then fed forward steadily until it has passed completely over the knives, finishing the movement with the aid of a push stick or pusher block. It is likely that the surface is now satisfactory, but if it is not the same surface is planed again. The timber is now turned through ninety degrees, and the surface which has just been planed is placed firmly against the fence. The wood may not be making contact with the table if it is badly out of square, but it is full contact with the fence that is needed. Maintaining this contact, the wood is given as many passes as may be necessary to produce a flat surface which rides on the table as its neighbour contacts the fence. If this process is continued so that the other two sides are planed in sequence, the resulting workpiece, when checked with a square, should prove to have four ninety degree corners. If this is not so, the fence is probably not square to the table, which can be discovered by using the square against table and fence. It is good policy always to check this before beginning planing operations.

Safety Points

The placing of the hands must be considered at all times, and nothing should be allowed to interfere with the concentration of the operator. A moment's inattention is all it takes, and it is important to remember that hands should never be passed over the cutter block, even with the guards in place.

PLANER THICKNESSERS

The real difference between surface planers and planer thicknessers, apart from the length of the knives, is that thicknessing cannot normally be performed on a surface planer. Some of them do have attachments which enable this to be done, but they are not really suitable for anything other than occasional hobby use.

The machine shown in most of the illustrations is the De Walt planer thicknesser, which has established itself firmly as a favourite among home woodworkers, and is capable of an excellent performance if kept in adjustment. I have been using this machine on a regular basis for some time, and in spite of my naturally critical attitude towards woodworking machinery, I have found it very satisfactory indeed. It is worth noting that a mortising attachment can be fitted to this planer, and while not suitable for heavy production runs in a commercial situation, for which it is not designed, this attachment is well worth its money, and certain to delight the hobbyist.

Construction of Thicknessers

When the proud new owner examines the thicknessing system on the machine, there is often a sense of gloom, in that it all appears to be very complex. This is not in fact so, and the thicknessing of timber is a very straightforward operation. One or both of the surfacing tables has to be lifted, and for this purpose they are hinged at one side. Usually there will be some provision for locking them in the raised position, so that they cannot fall while the tool is in use. Note that stops are fitted to most planer thicknessers to ensure that the tables are returned to exactly the right position when surfacing is resumed, and that the machine must be kept free of dust and chippings around these stops. With the table, or tables in the case of the De Walt 1150 shown here, in the raised position, most of the mechanism can be seen clearly.

There will be two rollers, one in front of and one behind the cutter block. The front one has ribs, which are often helical, and is the powered feed roller which takes the material through the machine. The rear roller is normally faced with rubber or neoprene, and is known as the take off roller. The cutter block itself will be plainly visible, as will the very important anti-kickback fingers, which trail on the wood as it passes through, and prevent it from being rejected by the knives and flung back towards the operator. Additionally there will be a combined cutter guard and chip deflector, which must be in place when thicknessing.

Thicknessing

The process of passing timber through a thicknesser is very simple, but there are one or two points to watch. On many machines the feed roller can be engaged or disengaged, so that it

Twelve inch planer thicknesser as fitted to MiniMax C30 universal machine. The figure of twelve inches relates to the length of the cutter block, which is three bladed. Note thicknessing scale at left, and rise and fall control wheel for thicknesser table (bottom centre).

De Walt planer thicknesser in surface planing mode. Note fence and guard. Thicknesser table is fully lowered when surface planing, as shown here.

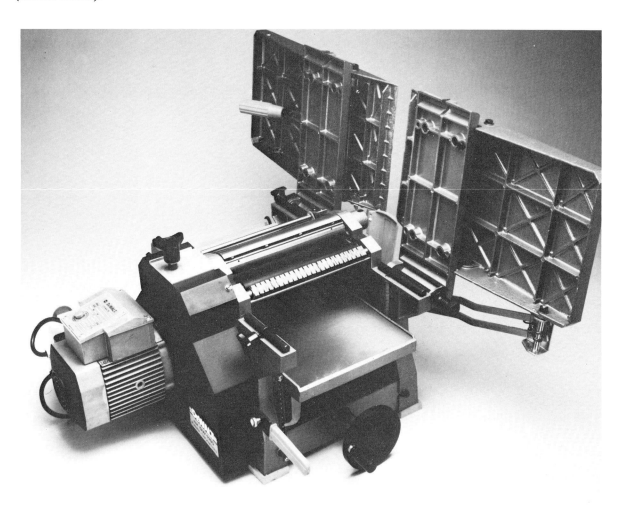

The De Walt planer thicknesser with surface planing tables lifted to show the thicknessing table and anti-kick-back mechanism.

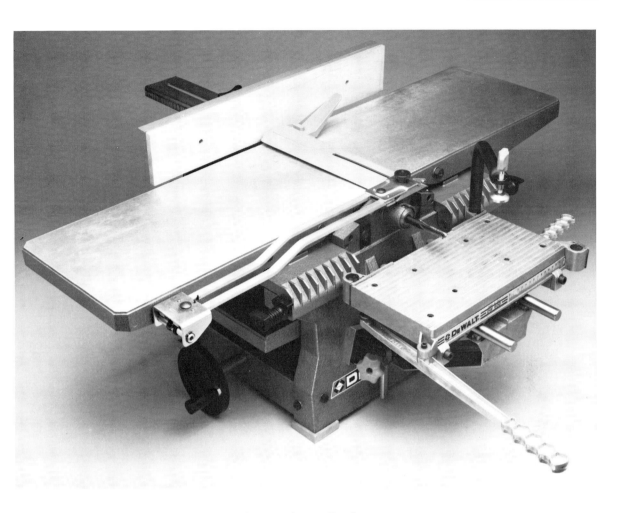

The De Walt planer thicknesser with mortising attachment fitted.

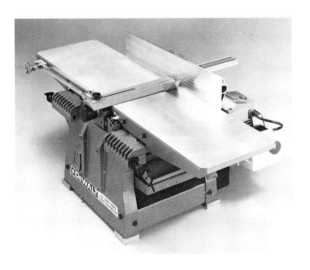

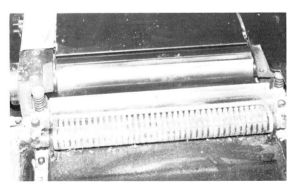

Cutter block and anti kick-back fingers of C30 thicknesser. When in use, these items are guarded by the chip deflector. Note Jacobs pattern chuck on end of cutter block, used for mortising and drilling.

The De Walt 1150 planer thicknesser, showing guard and fence, both adjustable to suit the job.

does not have to be rotating when it is not required, as in surface planing. It will therefore be necessary to engage it before thicknessing can be performed. Thicknessers can remove quite a lot of wood at one pass, but this is hard on the machine, and is not good practice. Several light passes are a far better idea.

There is likely to be a scale fitted to the machine for thicknessing, but these are awkward to use, and I rarely bother with them. It is best to check before inserting timber that it has both faces parallel in length. If it is thicker at one end than at the other, the thicker end must be inserted, or the wood will jam, and the machine may be damaged. Timber which is to be thicknessed should first be surface planed, and the planed surface should ride in contact with the table.

Many people are initially puzzled by the fact that when the timber is put into the machine it either will not enter, or nothing happens when it does. The answer to this is to put the timber in until it is under the feed roller, and wind the table up until the wood is taken through. It may be that no cut occurs, in which case the table is wound up a further quarter to half a turn, and the procedure is repeated until the knives cut.

One piece of timber should be fed to these machines at a time, it being bad practice to pass several narrow pieces of unequal thickness through together, except in the case of industrial machines, on which provision is made for this.

Another danger lies in attempting to thickness pieces of wood which are shorter than the width of the table. These are capable of rotating as they go through, and if they end up in a situation which presents them to the knives cross grained they may shatter and damage the planer.

The planer thicknesser has a thicknessing table below the cutter block, which can be raised and lowered by means of a handwheel, and when the tool is in use for surfacing this table should be at its lowest position. Many people complain that a build up of shavings occurs on the thicknessing table when surfacing, which is quite true, and these can cause problems in that they are flung out by the cutter block and cause annoyance to the worker. The best answer to this is to use a good dust extractor, with the end of the pipe positioned on the thicknessing table, clear of the knives. In the absence of such equipment the shavings must periodically be

Surface planing tables of De Walt machine are raised when thicknessing. Here the cutter block and anti kick-back system can be seen clearly.

Thicknessing is carried out on the De Walt with the chip deflector swung over to guard the cutter block. A locking system is incorporated to prevent the tables from falling.

The planer fence can be set at any desired position across the table, and the spring loaded guard provides full security. The thicknessing table is raised and lowered by means of threaded rods, one at each corner of the table. One of these is visible here (bottom left).

cleared by hand, but NEVER put a hand into this area while the planer is running. Before I had a dust extractor I kept a length of board handy to push the shavings out with, but now I work in luxury!

Planer thicknessers which are fitted with steel tables are very expensive, but they do present less resistance to the passage of the timber than do aluminium ones, and there may be problems on the latter type in the early stages with the wood sticking and being burned by the feed roller. This can be overcome quite easily, and the usual procedure is to 'feed' the thicknesser and surfacing tables regularly with wax, which reduces friction considerably, and there should be no further trouble.

Maintenance

Planer maintenance is really a matter of giving nuts and bolts an occasional check for tightness, keeping the knives sharp and correctly set, and cleaning the mechanism. The thicknessing table is raised and lowered by means of four threaded rods, one at each corner, which are driven by means of a chain and sprockets when the handwheel is turned. These should be inspected from time to time, and after cleaning they can be greased, or given a coat of machine oil. Never allow a planer to be lifted by its tables – this can be extremely bad for the machine, and happens to be a rather tempting practice.

Sharpening the Knives

Many owners make the mistake of removing knives from the machine when they have become blunt, and sending them away to be ground. This is expensive and unnecessary, and should only be done when the knives have been chipped by some metal object in the timber. They can be sharpened quite easily on most planers without removal from the block if the following procedure is adopted, but when this has been done a few times they will need slight raising in the block.

The first step in sharpening should be automatic, since it is the removal of the plug from its socket. The feed table is then lowered until it is approximately level with the bevel of a knife when the bevel is horizontal. A medium grade oilstone is now wrapped in paper, leaving a short section uncovered at one end, and oil is applied to the stone.

Final adjustment is now made to the table height, so that when the oilstone is flat on the table surface its uncovered section lies flat on the horizontal bevel. Care must be taken in this, or the sharpening may alter the angle of the bevel, which must be avoided.

The paper protects the table as the stone is passed smoothly back and forth along the knife, the cutter block being held firmly by its drive pulley. It is best to give each knife the same number of passes, and this 'touching up' of the knives will improve the performance of the machine enormously.

It is generally considered that planers of this kind should give around twelve thousand cuts per minute, which of course means that the ideal speed for a two-bladed machine is six thousand r.p.m., and that for a three-bladed one will be four thousand r.p.m. All this is fine, but it presupposes that the knife projection is exactly equal, and if one knife is high it will be doing all the hard labour while its fellows merely help to clear the chips. The performance of a planer can therefore drop dramatically if there is a high knife.

One final point in connection with the preparation of square stock is that the procedure for producing four right angled corners, as previously described, does not necessarily produce a piece of wood which has all sides of equal width. Those who have thicknessing facilities will normally surface plane two adjacent sides so that they are at ninety degrees to one another, then pass the wood through the thicknesser twice, presenting an unplaned side to the knives on each occasion. This, provided that the table is not moved between cuts, will give a true square, and is the method I always employ when preparing posts for the building up of woodturning blanks.

PORTABLE PLANERS

Small portable electric planers often appeal to beginners, who unfortunately expect more of them than they can give. For example, planers of this kind have cutters around two and a half inches long, and wide boards cannot be planed satisfactorily with them. The best way to understand this tool is perhaps to imagine it as a full sized planer which has shrunk to proportions which enable it to be held in the hand and used in an inverted position. This may seem odd, but it is a realistic view in the sense that these planers are made on a smaller scale but in almost exactly the same way as their larger brethren. If the planer is visualised upside down it will be noted that there is a feed table and a take off table, and that if a fence and guard were to be fitted there would be little other than size to distinguish the machine from large

planers. A control knob is provided at the front of the machine to move the front table up or down, so adjusting the depth of cut. It is usual to set this at about $\frac{1}{16}$ inch and leave it so.

The knives of hand planers are not normally honed *in situ*, as would be the case with bigger machines, but they are supplied complete with a jig, and sometimes a special oilstone. The blades are removed from the block and fitted into the jig, which ensures that as they are honed the angle of the bevel remains correct.

Elu hand planer, showing fence, and clip-on dust extraction unit. The metal carrying case is useful when these tools are used for on-site work.

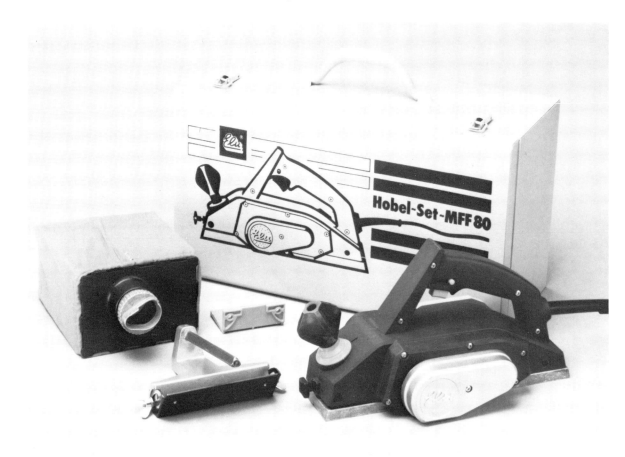

Applications of Hand Planers

Hand planers are used widely by builders for 'shooting' the bottoms of doors to provide the required clearance when fitting them, and they do a good job of planing suitably narrow stock. Wood being planed with these tools must however be securely clamped.

The only use I have been able to find for such a planer in the past is the cutting of rebates, which in the absence of a better tool they can do quite well. A guide fence is usually available, or provided with the tool, and this is set to give the required rebate width when run along the edge of the wood. A few passes will give the required depth, and the rebate is smooth and clean.

Underside view of small portable planer. Note the fence, and the cutter block mounted between two 'tables'. The smaller of these is the front table, and can be adjusted to alter depth of cut.

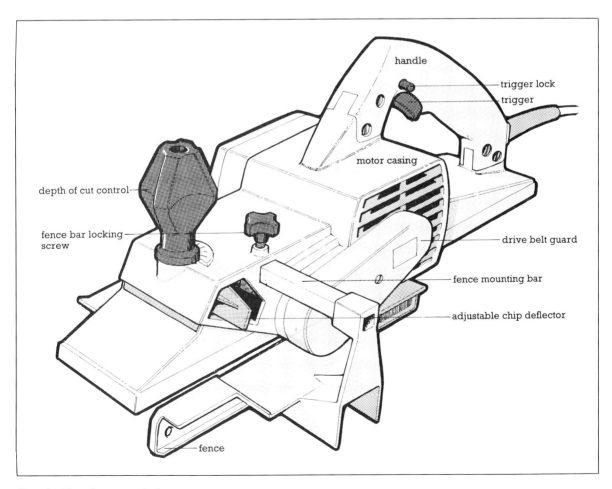

A typical hand operated planer.

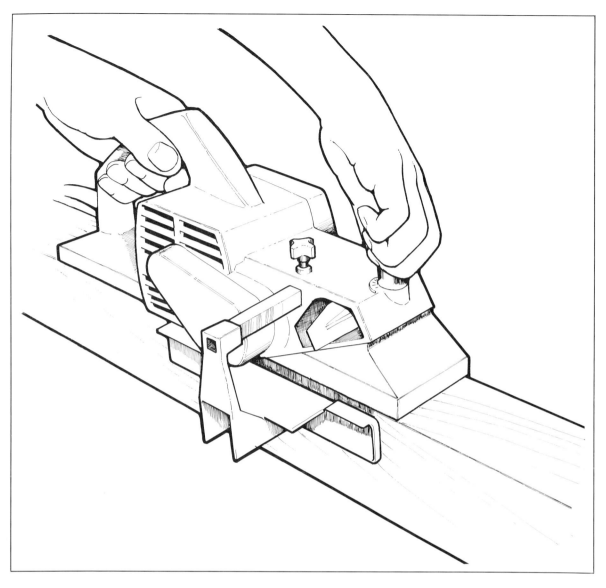

The hand-held electric planer does a good job on work up to the width of its cutters. It works best when set to remove about $\frac{1}{16}$ inch at a pass.

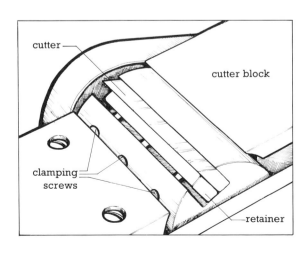

An inverted view of a portable electric planer showing the cutter installation.

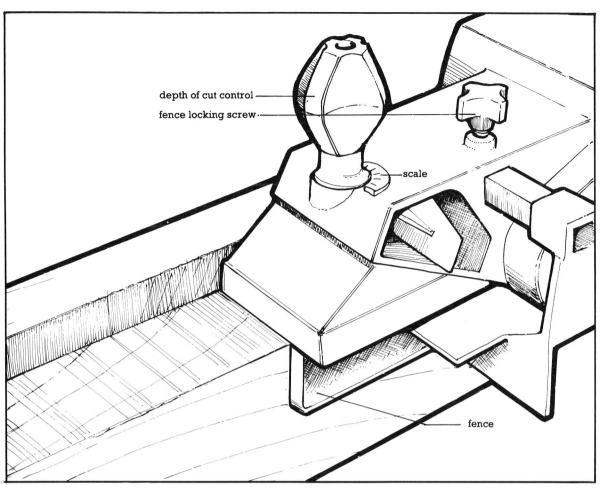

depth of cut control
fence locking screw
scale
fence

Hand held planers are useful for rebating. The rebate width is controlled by the fence setting, and the waste is removed by a series of passes.

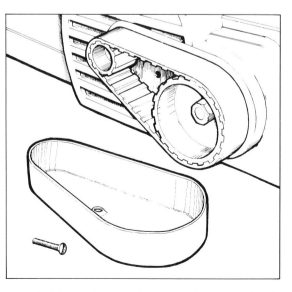

A typical toothed belt drive as used on many hand held power tools.

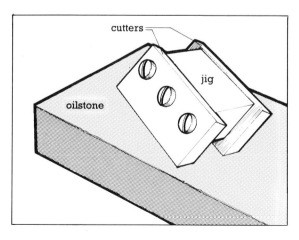

cutters
jig
oilstone

Most manufacturers of hand held electric planers provide a jig to enable the cutters to be honed without changing their bevel angles.

9
MORTISERS

Mortice and tenon joints are widely used in woodwork, and mortices can be cut by hand using a suitable chisel and a mallet, once the knack has been acquired. This is a pleasant occupation if time is not an important consideration, but where numerous mortices have to be produced a good mortiser or mortising attachment is well worth its cost. Like all good machines, these will permit rapid and accurate production in the hands of a skilled worker. The amount of skill required in the setting up and use of mortisers is not great, and an hour or two of trial together with a certain amount of error will pay dividends.

Types of Mortiser

There are two quite distinct types of mortiser, these being the hollow square chisel variety, known as the chisel mortiser, and the slot milling mortiser, which employs a rotary cutter. Chisel mortisers are not widely used by home woodworkers, largely because purpose-built machines are very expensive, usually extremely heavy, and not as simple to set up and operate as their rotary counterparts. Cutters for rotary mortisers are very cheap by comparison with the chisels and augers used in chisel mortisers, which can be an important factor where funds are limited, and a wide range of sizes is needed. The chisel mortiser does score heavily in one respect, however, which is that it can cut much deeper mortises, though these are seldom needed in home woodwork.

There is in fact a third type of mortiser which will cut very deep mortises indeed. This is the chain mortiser, which looks a little like a chain saw blade mounted in a stand, but its use is restricted almost entirely to industry.

Construction of the Slot Mortiser

The rotary machine, normally referred to as a slot mortiser, is the type preferred by hobbyists, partly for the reasons given above, and in view of the fact that it is frequently available as an attachment to other machines. The illustrations show slot mortisers fitted to the Mini-Max C30 universal machine, and to the De Walt planer thicknesser. In both cases the tool works well, but I normally find that with mortisers of this kind it is necessary to build a wooden sub

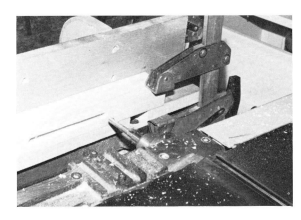

Set-up for mortising on the MiniMax C30 universal, using home-made sub-table with vertical fence to hold work. The planer block at the bottom of the picture will be covered by a guard before starting work.

table, which can be fixed to the table of the machine, to provide better support for workpieces. Many such machines do offer clamps to hold the wood, but frequently they are not as secure as they might be, and if the wood moves while it is being cut, the result can be disaster.

The cutter of a slot mortiser is held in a chuck similar to that used on an electric drill, this being fitted to the host machine, normally on the planer shaft. In such cases adequate guarding is provided by the manufacturers, and this MUST be used in accordance with the instructions supplied with it, so that the planer knives are fully guarded. In the interests of safety, the mortising cutter should be removed from the chuck when it is not required.

It is also worth noting that these cutters are designed for a specific direction of rotation, since on some machines they will be rotating clockwise as viewed from the operator's position, and on others the direction may be anticlockwise. There are two popular types of cutter, the more widely used being the variety which has two cutting edges, one of which carries sharp teeth, and the other is a knife edge. The alternative design has no teeth, but simply two straight cutting edges. Both are effective, but the former cuts more rapidly and with less build-up of heat. As with all cutters used in woodworking machines, these must be kept sharp, in order to avoid undue strain being imposed on the motor. Slot mortising cutters also need to have an end milling capacity, to enable them to enter the wood before being moved sideways to form a slot.

Assembly

The table is designed to provide movement relative to the cutter in both sideways and 'fore and aft' directions, and the height of the table relative to the cutter can be adjusted. There will also be a length and depth setting system, usually by means of stop rods fitted under the table, to limit its travel on its slides. These rods must be securely tightened once they have been adjusted, or they may be slowly knocked out of place during the mortising, thus creating inaccuracies.

It will be fairly obvious in view of all this that the wood has to be clamped securely to the table, correctly presented to the cutter, and there must be no possibility of the workpiece moving during the cut. Unfortunately the clamping de-

vices provided on some mortisers are not entirely satisfactory, and if this proves to be the case a wooden sub table should be bolted to the table of the mortiser, with an adjustable wooden fence, so that workpieces can be placed on the table and clamped to the wooden fence by means of G clamps.

Operation

The operation of this type of machinery should present no real problems, assuming the mortiser in question to be a well designed and

Once the guard is in position the mortise can be cut. Note that the planer knives and the mortiser chuck are well covered. Mortises are cut by a series of shallow passes, and heavy cuts must never be attempted.

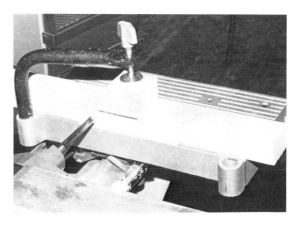

Mortises are cut with timber clamped firmly to table by a hold down arm, and aligned by means of a lip at the front edge of the table. Length and depth stops are set, and a trial mortise is cut. Note use of block of scrap timber to avoid marking workpiece.

made example. Cheap versions tend to have flimsy tables and table supports, together with inadequate and inefficient clamps to secure the workpieces. This kind of construction naturally leads to frustrating inaccuracy, and low quality machines are best avoided. Table movement must be smooth and precise, without 'slop' or wobble in the mechanism. An intending purchaser will also be well advised to examine the system provided for controlling the length and depth of mortises, which should be positive in operation, accurate, and capable of quick and simple adjustment.

Once the machine has been set up and thoroughly checked, a cutter can be fitted securely in the chuck, and some trial mortises can be made in scrap material, which will enable the user to get the feel of the tool, and to check its accuracy. A fairly wide range of cutters is available, in various diameters, but most home users will manage quite well with only two or three of these, three eighths or half inch diameter being very popular.

There are two approaches to mortising with these machines, one being to mark out each mortise carefully on the wood and to perform the cutting operation by eye, which is perhaps the better method if only a few mortises are required. The alternative is to make a simple jig to fit onto the table of the machine, making use of stop blocks to position the workpieces. Once such a jig has been made up and tested for accuracy, any number of mortises of similar length and depth can be cut without marking their positions on the wood beforehand, provided of course that the dimensions of the workpieces do not vary. The stop blocks should be clear of the table surface, to prevent the accumulation of wood chips or dust which might spoil the accuracy of the work.

Mortiser Tables

Mortiser tables are operated by means of levers, one moving the table from side to side, the other taking it forward or back, and once the workiece is securely clamped in position, at a

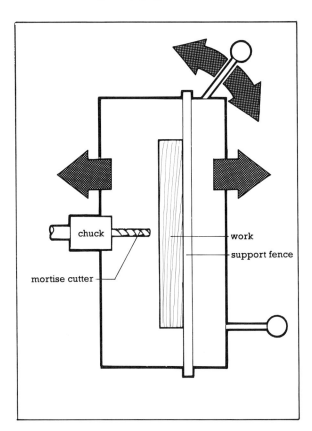

The lever moves the table and wood forward or backward in relation to the mortise cutter. The depth of cut at each pass must not be greater than the cutter diameter.

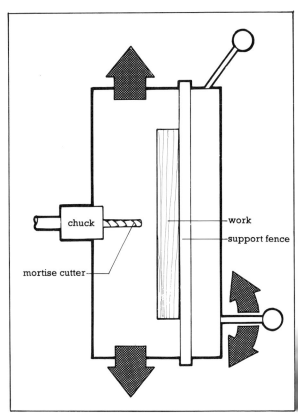

The traverse lever moves the table and work left or right relative to the cutter. The length and depth of mortise can be set by means of stop rods below the table.

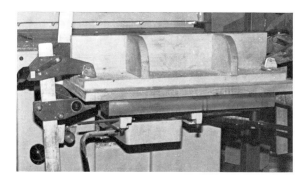

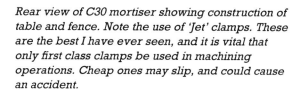

Rear view of C30 mortiser showing construction of table and fence. Note the use of 'Jet' clamps. These are the best I have ever seen, and it is vital that only first class clamps be used in machining operations. Cheap ones may slip, and could cause an accident.

In this illustration the guard for the planer knives has been omitted for clarity, but must always be in place when mortising. Mortise cutters should be removed from the chuck as soon as mortising is finished, not left in place when the planer is used, or a serious accident will sooner or later result.

height which positions the cutter correctly in relation to its face, the stop rods are set to give the exact length and depth of cut required. Once the knack of using this type of machine has been acquired, mortises can be produced very quickly, but certain factors should be observed.

The correct set-up when cutting a mortise is shown here, with the planer knives fully guarded. Two small blocks can be seen, near the ends of the front edge of the table, secured by Allen screws. These are the mortise length stops, and can be adjusted by releasing the screws and sliding them to the required positions.

Depth of Cut

Rotary mortising cutters must never cut deeper than their own diameter at one pass. If they are made to do so they will not work efficiently, and may snap under load, which could be dangerous. The correct procedure is to remove a little wood with each successive pass, feeding the table and workpiece forward at the end of each stroke until the depth stop brings the cutting to a halt. When the cutter is used to form a mortise which is the same width as the cutter diameter, cutting can take place in either direction. If however it is necessary to enlarge such a mortise by raising or lowering the table, then repeating the cutting procedure, attention must be paid to the common woodworking machinery requirement for timber to be fed against cutter rotation rather than with it. Cutter breakage can result from an incorrect feed direction.

Provided that the direction of feed rule is observed, it will be clear that the slot mortiser can be used for cutting rebates, or even tenons, if the wood is securely clamped and a little is removed at each pass.

Types of Cut

One difference between slot mortisers and the chisel versions is that a mortise cut with a rotary cutter is necessarily round ended, whereas that produced by a chisel is square. This is not a problem, since the ends of slot mortises can be squared with a sharp wood chisel, or the corners of the matching tenons can be rounded over on a sander. Chisel mortisers are not as popular with hobbyists, and this is due in part to the fact that they are more troublesome to set up, and most workers have difficulty in sharpening the chisels, which are hollow square sectioned, and are bevelled on their inside edges. They operate by means of a special auger fitted inside them, which drills a hole in the wood, the chisel following and trimming the edges. Large chisels used in hard timbers require a great deal of force in operation, but the smaller ones work quite well.

Mortising Attachments

When an attachment for slot mortising is purchased for a powered machine, it must be fitted carefully, in exact accordance with the instructions, and when this has been done, a check should be made to ensure that full and free movement of the table can be achieved, and that all nuts and bolts have been sufficiently tightened.

Chisel mortisers are not available as attachments for other machines, with the exception of the bench drill or pillar drill, and a chisel mortising attachment is shown in place on one of these on page 19. A bench drill needs to be very substantially made to work like this, because considerable strain can be imposed when driving large chisels into hard wood, and dedicated chisel mortisers are expensive because they take this into account.

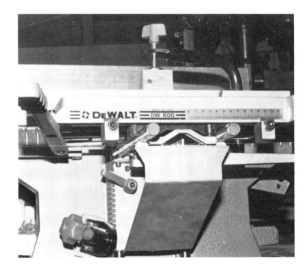

De Walt DW600 mortising attachment mounted on De Walt 1150 planer thicknesser. Handle at left moves table sideways, that at the right moves table towards or away from the cutter. Control knob at bottom left adjusts table height relative to cutter, and two small levers are provided to lock the table firmly in place.

10
THE PORTABLE ROUTER

Routers are now to be found in regular use in many home workshops. Technological advances have also occurred, rendering them easier to use, and greatly increasing their versatility and accuracy, yet many owners do not fully appreciate the capabilities of the machine, and so fail to derive full benefit from it.

Construction

In basic terms a router is a very high speed motor, contained in a specially designed casing, and driving a shaft to which is attached a chuck which enables suitable cutters to be gripped. This casing is attached to a flat circular plate known as the sole plate, and the casing can be adjusted vertically in relation to the sole plate in order to provide the required projection of the cutter.

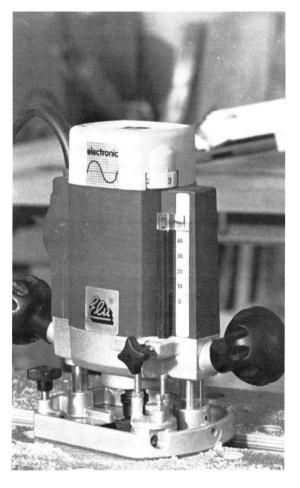

MOF98 router with guide fence removed. Note speed control knob (top right), and depth scale with marker. To the left of the scale is the adjustable stop rod which in conjunction with the turret head controls the depth of cut.

Underside view of Elu MOF98 router with guide fence attached. The fence, like the router, is beautifully engineered and very efficient.

Remember that the motor speed quoted by the makers will be the 'no load' speed, and refers to the free running state of the tool. During a cut the speed will be less than this, and it is important to listen to a router while cutting, in order to ensure that it is not overloaded. In a properly executed cut the speed of the tool is nevertheless high by comparison with other power tools, and this is one of the secrets of the router's success.

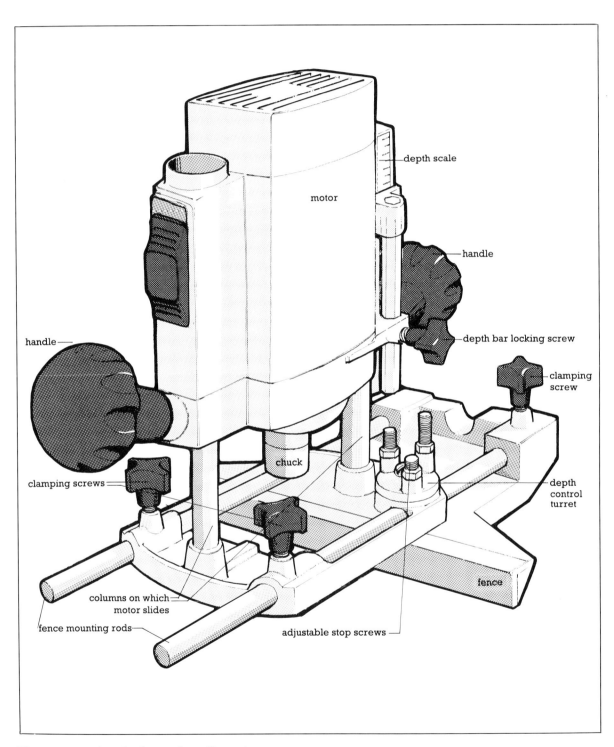

The component parts of a good quality router.

Reference to the drawings and photographs will help in following the various descriptions given here, and although the construction and use of the machine may at first appear complex, a week or two of experimenting on scrap timber will show that this is not really the case.

Cutters

Because routers have achieved a high level of popularity, there is now a seemingly endless variety of cutters, which can deter some woodworkers. It is not necessary however to buy all of them, or even half the range, and most home workers actually have occasion to use very few. Informative charts can be obtained from manufacturers, which provide drawings of the cutter shapes, and indicate their specific purposes, but cutter prices vary from quite cheap to phenomenally expensive, according to their shapes and to the types of steel used.

Some routers are now fitted with what is known as 'full wave' speed control, which enables the speed of the motor to be varied without loss of power, so that high speeds can be used with small diameter cutters, and the speed can be reduced when larger ones are fitted. As with a circular saw or a planer the important aspect of the matter is the tip speed of the cutter, which will vary with cutter diameter if motor speed remains constant.

One of the most significant changes in design has been the 'plunging' system, now incorporated into most models, and few people who

have given a fair trial to a plunging router would care to go back to the older designs. In these models the motor casing or 'router body' is attached to a spring loaded frame, and to the bottom of this frame is fixed the sole plate. A lever is provided in a convenient position, to permit the locking or unlocking of the plunge system. When the plunging mechanism is fully extended, the router body is at its maximum distance from the sole plate, and the cutter will be well clear of the bench on which the machine is standing. One big advantage here is that when the lever is pressed to release the plunge lock, the router can be pushed down onto a workpiece so that the cutter enters at ninety degrees to its surface. Another is that when a cut is finished the lever can be used to unlock the mechanism, and the router body allowed to rise, withdrawing the cutter from the work with no danger of its being tilted in the process and damaging the job. The cutter is automatically placed in a safe position by this process.

Early routers were something of a nuisance in some cases because the worker's view of the cutter was restricted. The modern machine, however, provides excellent visibility, and the design gives more room for spanners when cutters are being changed. In addition to this, safety is greatly improved by the fact that the rotating cutter need never be below the surface of the sole plate except during cutting operations, when of course the sole plate is on the work.

Choosing a Router

The routers shown in the photographs are from the highly respected Elu stable, and are current models. The version which is shown attached to a small radial arm saw is however an elderly Black and Decker HD1250 which has been in use for many years, and shows no sign of deterioration. I would strongly advise against the purchase of what may appear to be a cheap router, since this will almost certainly lead to disappointment. It is also a good idea to examine carefully the kind of advertisement which offers tools with a number of free cutters, since router cutters should only be obtained from reputable manufacturers, who invariably produce high quality examples. Cheap cutters will be blunt in a very short time, if they don't break first.

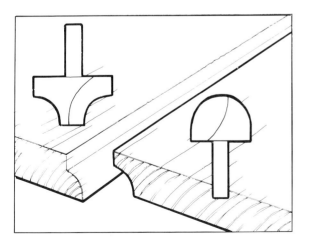

A useful pair of cutters for a router, which will produce joints for flap tables.

Assembly

Having unpacked the new router and fitted a suitable plug, the owner will be anxious to try it out, and the process of 'setting up', or preparing a router for cutting, is quite simple. Excellent facilities are now provided for depth setting and control, and once these are fully understood there should be few problems.

As with all power tools, the plug must be out of its socket when fitting or removing cutters. The first step is to slacken the chuck by turning the nut, and fit a suitable cutter. Assuming that the first trial will be in cutting a groove, a two flute cutter will be appropriate. The chuck nut is tightened by means of two spanners, one on the nut and the other applied to the motor spindle. This operation should not involve any force, or the chuck may be damaged. The router has a collet chuck, and different sizes of these can be obtained, to accept cutters with various shank diameters.

Depth of Cut

Depth of cut is preset by the user, and the initial stage is the slackening of the plunge lever, followed by pressing the router down until the tip of the cutter just touches the workpiece. The lever is now released, locking the machine in position, and attention is turned to the depth of cut scale. Note that some routers have a lever for clamping the plunge mechanism, but others may use a system which involves twisting one of the handles. The depth adjustment rod, which is fitted with a clamping screw, is now moved until

the distance between its tip and the top of one of the screw heads which protrude from the rotatable turret is equal to the desired depth of cut. The scale can be used to establish this, and the depth rod should be checked for tightness.

At this stage the plunging clamp is released, and the router is permitted to return to the top of its stroke. Since there are three adjustable screws fitted to the turret, it follows that three different depths can be preset, and selected by rotating the turret. As the operation in hand is the production of a groove, the side fence, which is standard equipment, will be used. This is attached to the router base by two rods, and should be moved to a position which will give a cut at the desired distance from the edge of the work against which the fence will run. The workpiece must be firmly clamped.

Operation

The router is now placed on the job, with the fence firmly against the edge of the wood, and is switched on. When the plunging action is used, the cutter will emerge from the base to the preset depth, and the cut is made by moving the tool along, keeping the base flat on the wood, and the fence against the edge. Deep grooves should be made by taking two or three cuts, the depth being increased each time by turning the turret.

When grooves are made on wide boards it may be inconvenient or impossible to use the side fence, and in such cases the router is guided by running its sole plate against a batten clamped

Black and Decker HD 1250 router mounted on a De Walt radial arm saw by means of a special bracket. This is an extremely efficient operating system.

Close shot of Elu router clearly shows turret type depth setting control with three stop screws, and the two pillars on which the router body is 'plunged'. The black screws on the left clamp the rods to which the fence is attached.

across the work. The batten, of course, must be so placed as to position the cutter at the desired point on the wood. The batten method can also be used when housings are cut across workpieces to take shelves.

The production of moulded edges to workpieces is a common operation, and some excellent results can be achieved if due care is taken. Most workers use cutters which have pins projecting downwards, the pins being known as guide pins. These are allowed to run in contact with the edge of the wood below the cut, but a little practice is necessary, since if they are pressed too firmly against the work the wood may be scorched, and if they are not kept in constant contact there will be irregularities in the finished job. An alternative to the pin guided cutter is the type which has small roller bearings instead of pins, although these are necessarily more expensive. They are easier to use, because the bearing rolls along the wood, and there is no friction. Very attractive mouldings can be produced, and cutters of this kind are commonly used for rebating, or for producing chamfers along edges.

The router is really a kind of small spindle moulder, and as with this machine it is desirable when moulding all four sides of a workpiece to make the cross grain cuts first, since the wood may spelch or break out at the end of these as the cutter emerges. If the ends have been cut before the sides, the side cuts will usually clean up any damage. The relationship between router and spindle moulder will be more apparent when we look at the use of the router in a purpose made table.

It is important for newcomers to routing to practise on scrap wood before attempting an important job, or lack of experience may cause the ruin of valuable timber. Those who wish to cut small rebates can do so using a straight cutter with the side fence, but the special rebating cutters which are available do a very good job with less fuss.

Carving

Woodworkers who have artistic talent, or who have relatives or friends who can draw, will find the freehand use of a router as a shape or pattern cutting tool very interesting, and quite easy to master. A small V or U shaped cutter is normally selected for this work, and the ubiquitous felt-tipped pen, preferably with black ink, will do a first class job on the wood in the right

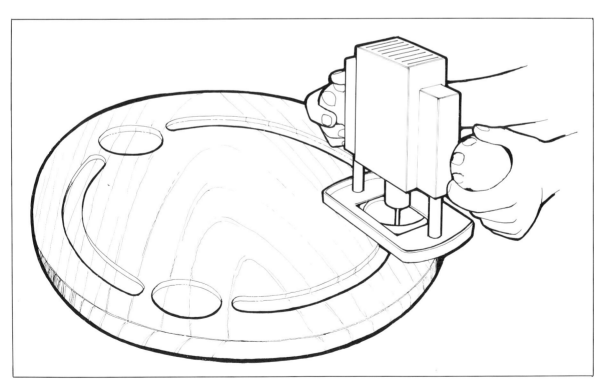

Some routing can be done freehand to marked lines, but this requires practice.

hands. Many carvers use routers to remove the background of relief carvings, which is a thankless task on a large piece. If this is done, however, it is necessary to fit two straight pieces of wood or metal across the router base, which are long enough to project outside the carving area. The router base does not then touch the wood, and a level surface results. Such pieces attached for this purpose are popularly referred to as 'skis'.

Working with Plastic

Those who use sheets of plastic material in the construction of kitchen furniture in the home workshop will know well that the accurate trimming of these materials when they have been laminated to a board is a trying business with hand tools. Routers excel in jobs of this nature, using specially designed cutters with tungsten carbide edges, which have roller bearings fitted below them. These cannot overcut, but the roller is guided by the edge of the board, so care must be taken to see that this is smooth, because if there are imperfections the router will copy them faithfully.

Accessories

Trammel arms, or as they are sometimes called, trammel bars, are very useful accessories for routers. If the trammel arm is of good quality, with a fine hardened steel pin, perfect circles can be cut into or through boards. The router is in fact the only portable power tool which will cut a perfect circle, which finishes with an edge which is smooth and true, requiring no further attention. Circles can be cut using a trammel arm with a jigsaw, but the results are inevitably inferior.

I use this method when making small tripod tables, which have turned central pillars, and legs which are first bandsawn and finally carved to shape. The turning of a really large diameter disc presents problems due to the significant speed differential between edge and centre, but the router does the work quickly and easily, and if the trammel arm setting is not changed, a moulding cutter can be fitted for the subsequent shaping of the edge.

For some jobs, like these table tops, it may not be considered desirable to use the pin of the

Underside view of optional control device. Trammel point is located in the small hole at extreme right, and is retracted into its housing when not required.

When routers are used for edge moulding they sometimes tilt, and so spoil the cut. The optional accessory shown here attached to the fence rods provides greater control, and also incorporates a steel trammel point, which can be lowered when required for use.

Dovetail cutting attachment for Elu routers, used with special dovetail cutters and a template guide. Note workpieces mounted ready for cutting. The joint is cut 'inside out'.

trammel arm into the workpiece. If this is so the customary method is to fix a thin scrap of plywood to the table by means of double sided adhesive tape. The pin is pushed into this, and the plywood can easily be removed when the job is done.

Unless the wood is very thin, no attempt should be made to cut a circle in one pass. The turret head should be used as described earlier, and the job done in three stages. The final stage should bring the cutter just fractionally through the material, and of course some waste board must be placed below the job.

Templates and Template Guides

The trammel arm is a worthwhile device, but there are limits as to the minimum diameter of circle which can be cut with these attachments. If smaller diameters are required, or there is a need to produce small circular recessed areas, the router is used with a template guide and a suitable template.

A template guide is a small plate which attaches to the sole plate of the machine, and which has a tubular section projecting downwards, surrounding the cutter. A little thought will reveal the fact that the cutter is distanced from the edge of the template by the thickness of the wall of the tubular projection, plus the gap between this projection and the cutter. When using the guide on the outside of a template, therefore, the template must be smaller than the required finished size of the job, and when working on the inside, as when cutting a circular recess, it must be larger. Templates must also be made with care, since any inaccuracies will be reproduced in the work.

If a template is only to be used on rare occasions, it can be made from good quality plywood, but this will be subject to deterioration through wear if used frequently, and the best substance I have encountered for template making is Tufnol, although some workers use perspex. Tufnol can be obtained in sheets through builders merchants, and I normally cut it to shape on the Hegner fretsaw (p. 123). Final smoothing is performed with files or rasps, and abrasive paper.

Many uses for templates will suggest themselves to the user as experience is gained with the router, but some obvious ones are recessing locks or hinges into woodwork, or cutting small mortises. The template is held firmly on the workpiece by the judicious use of double-sided adhesive tape, though this should be of a powerful variety such as is employed in securing heavy carpets. Some workers make templates which have a number of tiny sharp brad points protruding from them, which grip the wood.

Inverted Routers

A router inverted in a table is a light duty spindle moulder, and much of what I have written in respect of the spindle (see p. 118), as it is often called, will refer to the router when used in this way. It is quite possible for the home user to construct a table which will serve very well, but manufacturers such as Elu do offer first class tables, and the use of these will greatly simplify many router operations.

It should be noted that when a router is used in a table, and the edges of work are being machined, the wood must be fed against the rotation of the cutter, as would be the case in normal router work. A point which should perhaps be mentioned is that because of the very high speed of the router, the tool is rather noisy, and the volume and pitch of the noise is found trying by some operators. If long periods of routing are envisaged, it will be worth acquiring a pair of ear defenders, which are sold in good tool stores.

Using the Router Table

Router tables, like those of spindle moulders, have fences against which the material can ride

MOF98 router mounted in special table, for use as a small spindle moulder. This system greatly facilitates edge moulding and rebating operations.

during the cut, these being adjustable in position on the table. Some jobs may prove awkward to hold down to the table or against the fence, and use should therefore be made of springs, either as supplied by the makers, or constructed from plywood strips in the workshop. The latter are thin strips which have a wooden block attached firmly at one end, so that a clamp can be used to hold them in position. They are set so that the wood has to force them aside as it is fed through the machine thus being held against the fence or table.

Many jobs can be performed with the router in a table, and in some it is easier to move the timber relative to the router rather than to move the router along the wood, since there is no necessity for clamping the workpiece. Template routing of shapes is a good example, and in this operation the template runs against a roller bearing which is positioned above the cutter by means of an arm. The template is held on the upper surface of the wood by the usual adhesive tape, and the bearing is aligned with the edge of the cutter. When starting cuts of this kind the wood is pressed against a wooden stop block fixed to the table as it is fed to the cutter. As with spindle moulders this 'dropping on' action can be dangerous if the wood moves slightly with the direction of cutter rotation as it engages, and a kick back is likely. Once the cut has been started correctly however the bearing provides adequate support.

Routers attached to Radial Arm Saws

A router attached to a radial arm saw gives the best of two worlds, providing a cutter with a very high tip speed, ensuring clean work surfaces, and taking advantage of the extreme versatility of the radial machine. I have spent many long hours operating in this way on production work, and now keep my older De Walt in 'router mode' permanently.

Special brackets can be obtained for marrying the router to the radial, once the sawblade and guard have been removed, and they hold the router firmly so that it is free from vibration. Some operations are performed by moving the timber relative to the stationary router, and others by clamping the wood in place and pulling the motor complete with router along the arm. In the case of relief carvings, for example, the router can be fitted with a small straight cutter, and the tip of this is lowered into the workpiece by means of the radial's rise and fall control, to the required depth. The wood can then be moved around by hand until the background has been removed.

Moulding Edges

The moulding or rebating of edges is done by running the wood along the fence of the radial, with the cutter positioned as required, and it will be seen that by locking the motor in a selected position on the arm, with the cutter at the desired height from the worktable, grooving can be performed with ease. As with any other method, grooves should be taken with several light passes, lowering the arm a fraction between each, rather than in one heavy cut.

It is probably true to say that a well made router is as good as the person using it, and it lends itself to the invention of jigs, or the application of existing ideas. I hope very much that those who have never tried a router will be encouraged by reading this to do so, for I do not think that having once become accustomed to this tool they would ever wish to be without one.

Elu MOF98 'full wave electronic' variable speed router, mounted on a De Walt radial arm saw. The rotating cutter can be lowered to the required depth into the workpiece, which is then moved freehand. This system is used widely in making name boards for houses.

11
SANDERS

The process of smoothing wood by means of abrasive paper is still widely referred to as sanding, even though sandpaper as such is not used on machines. Observations on sanding in this book should therefore be taken as references to the use of various types of abrasive material.

Most woodworking projects will require or benefit from some form of sanding at certain stages, and there now exists quite a variety of machines for specific abrasive operations, these being known generically as sanders. Some of them will be well known to many readers, since they are used in home maintenance for sanding down paint, and in such pursuits as rust removal or car body repairs. Our concern here is with the application of the range of sanders to woodworking operations, where they are very efficient.

Powered sanders dramatically reduce the time taken, while still providing great efficiency, and are therefore a sound investment. Like all power tools, however, they must be properly maintained, kept in correct adjustment, and sensibly used.

Since they have no rotating knives or cutters they are less formidable to beginners, but they can cause injury if adequate care is not exercised, and some of them are quite powerful. If the instructions provided by the manufacturer are adhered to, a short period of practice on scrap wood will soon make the user feel at home with the tool, so there is no need for concern.

BELT SANDERS

Very large and powerful versions of this machine are available, but the smaller ones are in general easier to use, and more useful in the home workshop. Large belt sanders are very expensive, extremely heavy, and will remove wood at a phenomenal rate. Every example of the large belt sander I have used has contained a big paper capacitor, which has managed to absorb sufficient moisture in my somewhat damp workshop to cause it to explode with a bang, accompanied by a puff of black smoke. This, should it occur, is easily rectified by fitting a new capacitor, and in a dry environment it will not happen, but is perhaps worth a mention.

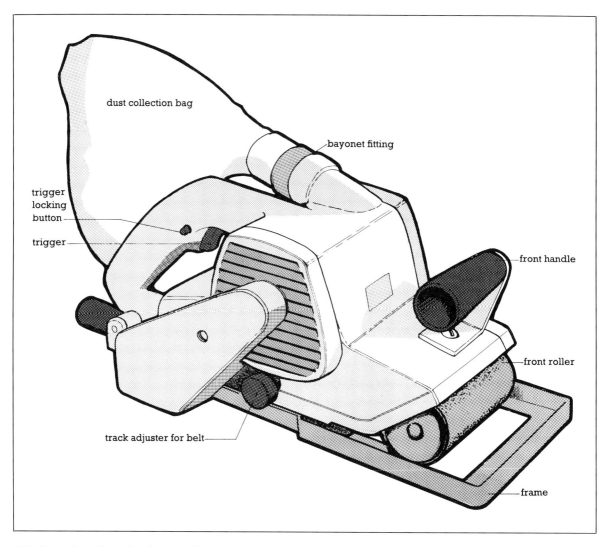

A belt sander with a depth control frame.

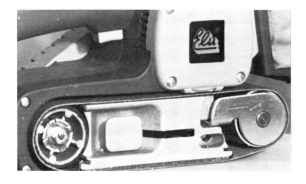

Elu MHB157 belt sander. A small machine, but extremely efficient, and better for normal home workshop use than heavier and more expensive versions.

Construction

Under the body of a belt sander, which contains the motor and drive mechanism, is a flat plate, at each end of which is fitted a metal drum. One of these drums is driven by the motor, normally by means of a toothed belt, and the other can be moved by altering the position of a lever, so that tension can be applied to or removed from the belt. When the machine is in use, the belt runs between the central flat plate and the wood, and the plate is spring loaded.

Assembly

The fitting and removal of belts is extremely simple and can be done very quickly, but it should be noted that belts for these machines have an arrow indicating the correct direction of rotation, and they must be fitted the right way round, or the joint in the belt will soon be damaged. A belt is fitted by operating the lever, which moves the front drum slightly to the rear. The belt is then slipped over the drums, and the lever is returned to its original position.

Dust Extraction

In all sanding operations consideration must be given to the disposal of dust, which is created in large quantities, and could present a health hazard. Modern belt sanders are fitted with dust extraction facilities which are reasonably effective, but I usually have the big dust extractor running as well. In the absence of one of these highly desirable machines, a good dust mask should be worn.

Track Adjusters

A further control on belt sanders which is simple to operate is the track adjuster. The belt should run centrally on the drums, so when a new belt is fitted the machine is started and a check is made to see if all is well. Usually it is not, so the adjuster is turned gently until the belt is running true. Checks should be made on this from time to time when working, since as belts stretch and wear the tracking will alter. In severe cases, where the belt is allowed to run for long periods when it has moved in towards the closed side of the tool, it may cut into the casing.

Operation

With the smaller versions a short period of practice will enable the user to control the tool and to produce very good results. As with all power tools, however, the machine must be running before it is brought into contact with the wood. Machines which are constantly started while standing on the wood will exhibit short motor life.

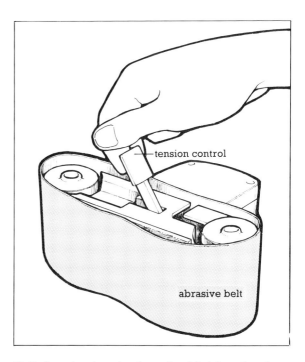

Belt changing is a simple and quick job on hand-held belt sanders.

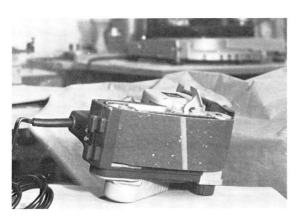

Underside of belt sander showing lapped joint in belt. Tension lever (just above belt) is pulled out as shown to permit belt changing, which is quick and easy.

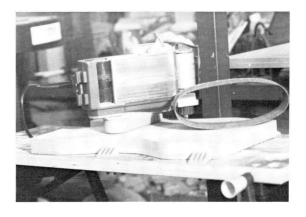

When the sanding belt is removed, the pulleys and the pressure plate can be seen. Front pulley moves back or forward when tension lever is moved.

Initial sanding can when necessary be done with a coarse abrasive belt, working down through the grades to arrive at the finest possible surface finish. In the early stages the tool is used either straight across the grain of the wood, or more usually at an oblique angle to the grain. The big advantage of a belt sander may not immediately be apparent, but the fact is that the abrasive grains move in straight lines, rather than following circular paths as is the case with disc sanders. It will therefore readily be appreciated that the tool can be used so that sanding is done along the grain, producing very good surfaces indeed with fine belts.

One big mistake which is common with newcomers to powered sanders lies in the application of downward pressure to the tool, in the hope of producing quicker results. This will normally overload the motor and reduce the sanding speed, whereas maximum efficiency is achieved by allowing the tool to operate under its own weight.

These machines should never be allowed to remain in one place on the work while running, or they will sink into the surface, producing ridges. Special frames can be fitted to some models to prevent this, but the answer is to keep the machine moving freely across the work surface all the time.

Another useful device, obtainable from some makers, is a metal frame which can be bolted to a bench. The sander is fitted into the frame in an inverted position, and can then be used as a stationary belt sander, the wood being moved around instead of the tool. This also enables curved work to be freehand sanded on the curved face of the front drum.

Awkward workpieces are easily handled in the Black & Decker Workmate, being clamped by the special plastic pads. Efficient clamping of timber to be belt sanded is sometimes difficult by other means, as the clamps tend to obstruct the free movement of the sander. Note dust extraction bag at front of tool.

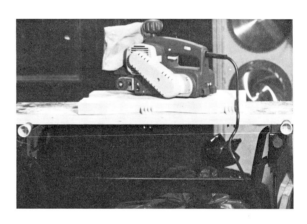

Drive belt of MBH157 runs inside plastic guard, transferring power from motor to rear pulley.

ORBITAL SANDERS

Orbital sanders are quite different in operation to belt sanders, although they are still capable of producing very fine surface finishes. One obvious difference when the orbital sander is in use is that it removes wood much more slowly than most other abrasive machines.

Construction

The construction of the tool is relatively simple, the motor driving a flat pad which carries the abrasive paper by means of an eccentric cam device. The pad moves at high speed with a

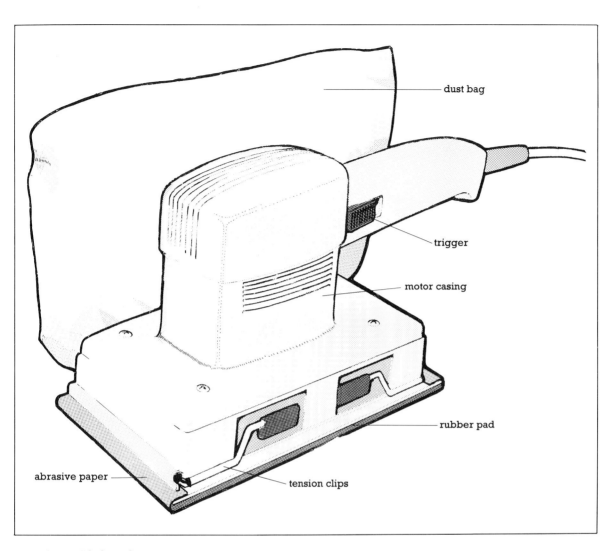

A typical orbital sander.

circular orbit as the tool passes over the wood, and when used for its true purpose as a finishing sander the machine is very useful.

Operation

The changing of abrasive sheets presents no problems: they are simply placed over the pad, and their ends are secured by small clips. It is, however, worth making an effort to get the abrasive paper as taut across the pad as possible. If there is too much slack the tool will have very little effect. As with the belt sander, a variety of abrasive paper grades can be used, and when the very fine type is fitted the work can be brought virtually to a polished condition. No downward pressure should be employed, as the machine moves under its own weight.

Large Elu orbital sander, used for matting down paintwork, or fine finishing on wood.

These tools often have dust extraction facilities, in which case there will be holes in the sanding sheets through which the dust can be taken under suction to a small bag attached to the sander.

Pad or Palm Sanders

Orbital sanders can be quite large, but a version which has become deservedly popular in recent years is the pad or palm sander, which is small, but effective. The Elu version of this, shown in the illustrations, is supplied with a special jig which allows the user to produce suitable sanding sheets complete with dust ex-

traction holes. These palm sanders are delightful little machines, and I find myself using one a great deal. They derive their name from the fact that the upper part of the body of the tool is designed to fit comfortably into the palm of the hand, and they do not have handles as such.

Speed Control

Some orbital sanders have facilities for varying the speed, in which case the lower speeds are used with coarse abrasive sheets for rapid stock removal, and the higher ones are reserved for finish sanding.

Pad or 'palm' sanders, by Black & Decker have orbital action, and are both efficient and pleasant to use. These are finishing sanders, and can give beautiful finishes when used with fine grades of abrasive paper. Note dust extraction bags.

DISC SANDERS

Disc sanders, as the name suggests, are basically just discs coated with abrasive paper, and

driven by some suitable workshop device. They can, for example, be fitted to the headstock of a lathe, to the motor spindle of a De Walt radial arm saw, into the chuck of a rotary mortiser, or as is often done, attached to the shaft of an old washing machine motor. They have their uses for relatively rough work, but there are some inherent problems.

Disc sanders are never really effective when used for finishing, since the grains of abrasive necessarily follow a circular path, and tend to leave scratches in the wood. A belt or orbital sander could be used to remove these scratches, but why not use the more efficient tool in the first place?

Another disadvantage, which is obvious when pointed out, is that the speed at which a given granule of abrasive travels will depend upon its distance from the centre of the disc, so although there may appear to be a wide area available for use, most of the work is done near the periphery.

Construction

Disc sanders are certainly useful for some operations, but in the main they can be regarded as a rough sanding aid. It is usual to fit a table at right angles to the disc, with its surface just a little below disc centre, to support work as it is sanded, and to present its edge at ninety degrees, or some other required angle, to the abrasive.

Most sander discs are of metal, but many workers make them from plywood or blockboard, and special adhesives are available for attaching the abrasive paper to the disc. These are designed to facilitate the removal of a worn out disc, and it is a mistake to use ordinary adhesives, which can make such removal extremely difficult. Some of the special adhesives seem unnecessarily expensive to me, and I frequently use rubber solution, which can be obtained from car accessory shops.

Using the Disc Sander

One of the most common, and effective uses of disc sanders is in trimming work which has been cut on the bandsaw. This cutting is normally done fractionally outside the marked lines, and provided that the edges of the workpiece are either straight or convex, they can be trimmed very simply on this type of sander. I much prefer, particularly where a large number of pieces have to be processed, to use a router in conjunction with a template guide, which is fast, accurate, much less dusty, and leaves a perfect finish on the edges.

Note that the abrasive grains are moving upwards on one side of the disc, and travelling down towards the floor on the other. The 'down side' of the disc is used, so that the work tends to be held down on the table. In the early stages of using this kind of equipment, many people find that they are having trouble with burning of the wood, and a sense of feel has to be developed with practice before the correct amount of material to disc pressure can accurately be judged. Another problem is that the discs will rapidly become clogged with wood fibres, especially when softwoods are being sanded. This can be removed quite easily by pressing a piece of hard plastic hosepipe against the rotating disc. This is done on the downward moving side, the end of the pipe being supported on the table and moved forward to contact the disc. It is also possible to purchase special liquids in which abrasive material can be washed to remove detritus of this kind, but these are quite expensive, and I never bother with them.

SANDING ATTACHMENTS

Finally we have the large family of small sanding attachments, designed for use in hand held electric drills, and in a wide range of other machines. To cover each one of these completely I would need far more space than is available, but it is certainly worth knowing the specific purposes for which each type is best suited.

The Rotary Pad Sander

One interesting idea which has come to the fore in the past few years is the use of a small pad sander in an electric drill or in conjunction with a flexible drive shaft, to finish off the insides of turned bowls. The sander can be used on the outside if desired, but it is the inside of a bowl which causes most trouble where beginners are concerned. The process looks as though it ought to be dangerous, but in fact it is not, and there is no doubt about its effectiveness.

The pad sander is a small disc sander consisting of a metal disc, to which is attached a shaft to fit into the drill chuck. A pad of foam rubber is provided on the face of this disc, together with a number of Velcro sections. The sanding discs themselves are backed with Velcro, and so can be fitted or removed quickly and without difficulty. As with all such sanders, the abrasive is presented to the work at a slight angle, so that only a part near the edge is used.

The actual process of sanding a bowl with this type of tool is quite simple. The lathe is run at its normal speed, which will depend upon the size of the bowl, and the sander is brushed back and forth across the wood, working ONLY on the side of the bowl which is travelling downwards. Very fine grades of abrasive are employed, and the results are normally very gratifying.

The Foam Drum Sander

The foam drum sander is quite a different beast, and has been with us for a very long time. One of its advantages will immediately be apparent, this being the fact that the abrasive can be made to work along the grain of the wood. Another is that burning of the timber is extremely unlikely to occur, which is more than can be said for many sanders. This tool is also versatile, being suitable for sanding either flat or curved work.

There is a metal central boss with a shaft to fit a chuck, and around the boss is a thick layer of soft foam rubber, or some similar substance. There is a screw at the centre of the boss, which when slackened will permit an abrasive sleeve to be fitted over the foam. The screw is then tightened, and the tool is ready for use. It should be applied lightly to the wood, and if too much pressure is used the belt may fly off, but this is unlikely to be a problem other than in the early stages.

Users will quickly work out ideas of their own for employing these sanders on specific jobs. I have used them in rotary mortisers for surface sanding, feeding the wood under the drum, on the mortiser table, against the direction of the abrasive. I have also found them useful when attached to a pillar drill, or in a chuck on a radial saw motor.

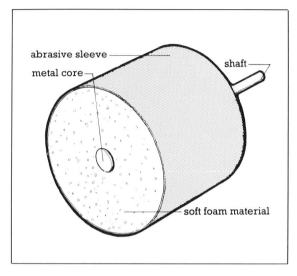

Foam drum sanders are now popular for use with electric drills in general sanding operations.

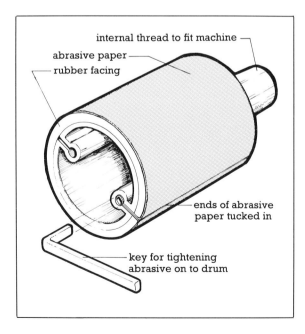

Small drum or 'bobbin' sanders like this are a great help on many jobs. They can be used with a bench drill, radial arm saw or a spindle moulder.

Bobbin Sanders

Bobbin sanders, though vaguely reminiscent of drum sanders, are in fact quite different. They are available as accessories for several type of machine, good examples being the spindle moulder and the De Walt radial arm saw. Woodturners often make their own wooden versions, covering them with foam rubber sheet before fitting the abrasive paper, and use them for sanding edges of curved work such as the legs of a wine table, or for sanding the faces of such legs to a concave curve to fit the central stem.

The type of bobbin sander likely to be found in a tool store has a layer of rubber over which the abrasive sleeve fits, and there is a nut or screw in the end of the sander which will expand or contract the rubber when tightened or loosened. The obvious disadvantage of this system is that one is committed to purchasing ready made abrasive sleeves of the correct size. The construction of the type supplied for the De Walt radial is different, and permits the user to cut small sheets of abrasive material and to tuck the ends into a slot, where they are held by a simple mechanism.

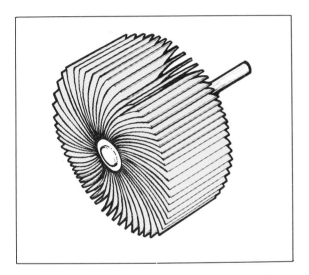

A flap sander, normally used in an electric drill and capable of producing fine finishes when operated with the grain of the wood.

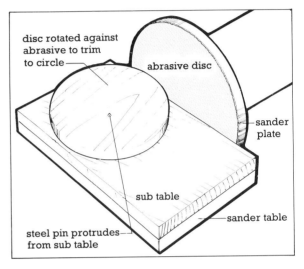

Machine mounted disc sanders are good for trimming off edges, with the aid of a home-made sub table like the one shown here. Wooden discs, such as wheels for toys, can be trimmed exactly to size and shape.

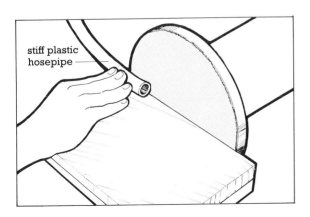

Stiff plastic hose brushed against 'down' side of sanding disc will clean the abrasive paper.

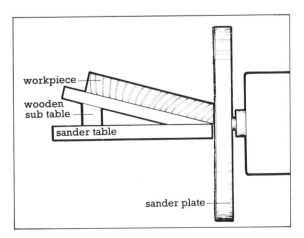

Angle sanding with a disc sander requires either a tilting sander table, or a home-made wooden sub table on which the work can rest.

Bobbin sanders are not as flexible as their foam drum brothers, and wood must therefore be applied lightly to them or burning will occur.

Flap Sanders

Flap sanders are used mainly for contour sanding in woodworking operations, and are simple little devices which do work quite well if applied lightly, with a brushing action. They will readily burn the wood if the abrasive is fine and the pressure too great. They consist of a number of flaps of abrasive which have one end free and the other embedded in the central core of the sander. In most cases they are used in electric drills, with the shaft of the sander gripped in the chuck.

Abrasive Materials

Abrasive materials in general woodworking use by home workers are aluminium oxide, which comes in a variety of colours, and garnet, which is orange. Sandpaper as such is unsuitable for power work since it is not sufficiently strong. Sheet material is normally paper backed, whereas belts are backed with cloth, and if used with care will last for quite a long time. Abrasive belts should not be discarded because they are worn, unless badly so. They will usually still do useful work, but not with their original speed. Abrasive materials are available in 'open coat' or 'closed coat' form, the former being preferable in most cases, since closed coat paper clogs with dust rapidly, and is more inclined to burn the wood. All abrasive paper or belting must be kept dry, or dried before use, because damp cloth or paper backed abrasive materials will clog with astonishing speed.

12
LATHES

The craft of woodturning was dormant for some years between its death as an apprenticed trade and its renaissance as a leisure and small business activity, and the majority of equipment on sale today is aimed at home users. As is fortunately the case with many other crafts, interest in woodturning has been growing considerably year by year, due in part to its therapeutic nature, and to the fact that it can form a self-supporting hobby or a means of making a living.

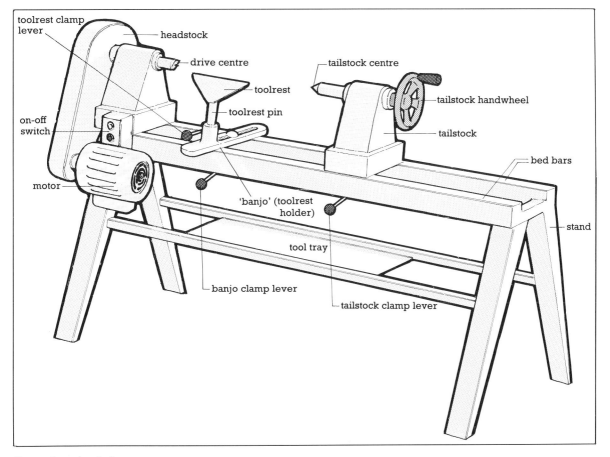

A woodturning lathe.

The rise in interest in the craft has meant a growth of manufacturers of lathes, tools, and accessories, and there is now a plethora of equipment to tempt the hobbyist. The newcomer to the craft must be wary when setting up a workshop for turning. Some lathes now being made are virtually rubbish, and the same can be said in the field of ancillary equipment. This is possible because the market is catering very largely for the absolute beginner, who is usually unable to make sound judgements in the absence of basic knowledge. This may be immoral, but it is sadly true.

How, then, is the novice to cope with this situation? The problem is exacerbated by the fact that the people who sell lathes are not usually woodturners, and they want to achieve a sale of a machine which they stock. In this chapter, therefore, I will explain the nature of the various lathes and types of equipment, and offer the same sort of advice as I have given to the several thousand students I have taught in the past twenty years. It is necessary to know what one is looking for if there is to be any chance of finding it.

It must be said at once that there are many good lathes, and from the viewpoint of the home user they do not have to be expensive. A wood lathe is a very simple tool, which merely serves to rotate the timber so that it can be cut and shaped with the correct tools by means of manual dexterity and skill. A lathe which has cost over two thousand pounds will do no more.

Construction

In general terms the construction of a wood-turning lathe, whatever its cost, is as follows. There will be a headstock, which is the part of the lathe which supports the driven spindle, and permits its rotation about its longitudinal axis, without other significant movement. This means that the headstock must be sturdy and rigid, and that the bearings which carry the spindle must be sufficiently heavy and of high quality. The spindle itself protrudes from the right hand side of the headstock, and on some lathes it also extends from the opposite side, so that large diameter turning can be undertaken without obstruction from the lathe bed. This system is not universal, and other approaches will be discussed, but lathes which are designed in this way are described as having out-

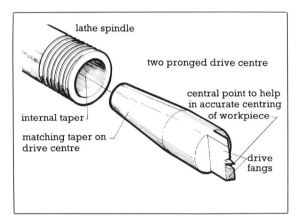

International standard 'Morse' tapers are used on head and tailstocks of good quality lathes to hold drive or tailstock centres, drill chucks, etc.

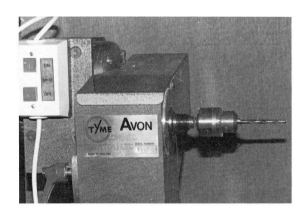

The very popular medium priced 'Avon' lathe is shown here with a Jacobs pattern chuck fitted to its headstock mandrel. For those with no alternative, such as a bench drill, the lathe can provide an efficient and accurate drilling system.

Here the headstock of the 'Avon' lathe is shown swung round through ninety degrees to face the operator. This permits the turning of large diameter discs, without obstruction from the lathe bed.

board turning facilities. One disadvantage is that several feet of workshop space must be reserved to the left of the lathe to provide room for the operator when turning outboard. Expense will also be incurred because the thread cut on the spindle has to be right handed on the right hand end, and left handed on the other. This means that chucks and faceplates will have to be duplicated if they are to be used in both locations. Further expense is involved in the fact that suitably heavy equipment for outboard turning, to support a tool rest holder and tool rest, must be fitted both inboard and outboard.

The end, or ends, of the spindle, apart from having a thread for the fitting of accessories, are on the better lathes tapered internally to an international standard known as Morse. Smaller lathes have a number one internal Morse taper, but the average lathe today is fitted with number two, which is thicker. Number three Morse tapers are to be found on some old lathes, but there is no real need for them, and they require a large diameter spindle. The advantage of an internal taper of this nature is that since it is machined to an international standard, an owner is able to make use of equipment made by other manufacturers.

Fittings

The fitting most commonly used in the spindle has a mating Morse taper, and is known as a drive centre, or driving centre. Its purpose is to penetrate a short distance into the end of a workpiece so that it can transmit the driving force provided by the motor to the wood. These

Strength and solidity are the hallmarks of the MiniMax T120 lathe, as shown in this photograph of the front bearing and spindle nose.

centres have a central point, which helps in positioning the workpiece in the machine, and they are provided with a number of driving fangs. Centres intended for the driving of very thin work have four fangs, so that two will necessarily cross the grain and help to reduce the wedge action of the centre, which might otherwise split the wood. General purpose drive centres have two fangs, but the wrong type is frequently fitted to new lathes, in which case two of the fangs can be ground away.

Lathe Beds

Lathe beds have been made in so many shapes that I can only speak of them here in broad terms. The lathe bed can be considered as either a single metal bar, or a pair of metal bars, which are likely to be round, square, or rectangular in section. Its purpose is to support the tool rest holder, (generally known as a 'banjo') and the tailstock, and to permit each of these fittings to be positioned and locked in place where required. The lathe bed must be sturdy, or there will be flexing and vibration, both being highly undesirable. The main features to look for in a lathe bed are strength, and ease of movement of fittings.

The tailstock is similar to the headstock in that it carries a spindle, which is internally tapered to match that of the headstock so that a centre can be fitted to support workpieces. The tailstock spindle is known as the poppet barrel, and can be projected from or withdrawn into the tailstock casing by means of a handwheel. A small locking lever is provided to lock the barrel, and a further lever is available for locking the tailstock in any selected position on the bed. The sturdiness and quality of the tailstock must equal that of the headstock.

Toolrest Holders

One toolrest holder is always provided, although some makers fit two, so that long toolrests can be used. Banjos have locking levers to clamp them in position, and the banjo itself should be long enough to permit it to be moved forward when large diameter cylinders are turned. Some cannot be moved far enough because they are too short, so the toolrest cannot be positioned for large cylinder work. The banjo has a vertical portion in which is a hole of suitable size for the pin of the toolrest itself, and a clamping device to permit the toolrest to be set at a desired height and locked.

Toolrests are devices upon which the tools are placed for turning, and their design, or rather the lack of it, is a constant source of annoyance to woodturners. Frequently the toolrest shape appears to have been chosen for aesthetic rather than functional reasons, which is unfortunate since when the turner has acquired sufficient knowledge he or she will throw the thing away and have a functional one made locally. Badly shaped toolrests can inhibit or even prohibit free movement of the tools.

Speeds

A range of speeds is provided by means of a system of stepped pulleys, usually giving four or sometimes five speeds spaced between around four or five hundred up to approximately three thousand r.p.m. The lathe is powered by an electric motor which should be of the totally enclosed induction variety. For home users a half horsepower motor is normally adequate, but three quarter or even one horsepower may be provided.

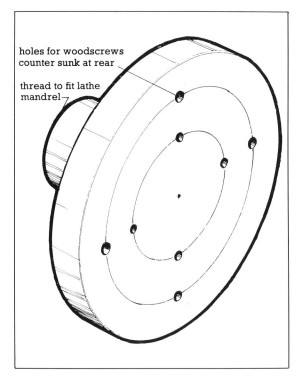

A steel faceplate.

Stands and Benches

Some lathes can be purchased with stands, but many people construct wooden benches for their machines. In either case the lathe should be set up so that the drive centre is approximately at elbow height for the user, which will avoid the back pains often derived from using lathes which are too low. Some manufacturers supply stands which are far too flimsy, although those for the MiniMax lathes shown here are excellent.

Turning Between Centres

The three main forms of woodturning are known as turning between centres, faceplate work, and chuck turning. Typical work between centres would be the making of balusters for staircases, table lamps, furniture legs, or anything which is essentially made from a 'stick' or piece of wood in which the grain runs lengthwise. Faceplate work includes the very popular production of bowls, dishes, platters, and the like, all of which are normally made from discs, and chuck work covers the production of smaller discs in various forms, together with such items as goblets, tankards, vases, and other hollowed items.

Faceplate Work

A faceplate is a metal disc in which several holes are provided for the passage of screws to hold the work. Many are unfortunately made from alloy, which is light and soft, and easily distorted by screwing to wood which is not truly flat. These have rims to stiffen them. Steel faceplates are far better, though they must be protected from rust. A faceplate has a central boss in which a thread is cut to fit the lathe spindle.

Chuck Turning

The range of chucks for woodturning has increased dramatically in the past ten years or so, but not all of those now offered for sale are desirable. The term 'chuck' is used to describe small fitments designed to hold wood when the tailstock is not in use, the work almost invariably being supported by the chuck alone, so the importance of good ones is obvious.

Woodscrew Chucks

Most workers have two woodscrew chucks, which are like tiny faceplates with a woodscrew projecting from the centre. Common sizes are one and a half inch and two and a half inch diameter, the larger one often having holes drilled near the periphery for extra screws to be fitted. These have been in use for many years, but they are losing ground now because of the introduction of what are known as chuck systems, universal chucks, multi-purpose chucks, and so on. By far the best example of these, in my opinion, is the Multistar Duplex system, which is very sophisticated, and beautifully engineered, which I have tried to describe here. It should be noted that chuck systems can cost up to about £300 if all the range of accessories is purchased. For most workers, however, this is unnecessary and not desirable, but fortunately there is a more sensible approach.

Woodscrew chucks are designed to hold small discs, or blocks of wood up to three inches or so in length. A hole of suitable size is first drilled in the piece of wood to be turned, which is called a blank, and this is then screwed onto the chuck until it is tight against the chuck face. They work well on discs, but care is needed when learning to turn blocks, since the retaining screw is in end grain, and has less holding power than when into face grain as is the case with a disc. The screws fitted to woodscrew chucks are ordinary woodscrews, and can on most chucks be removed when worn and new ones can be put in.

Most universal chucks or chuck systems include among their numerous attachments some form of woodscrew chuck, but these systems offer a wide variety of ways of holding wood, most of which will give greater support, and permit the turning of longer workpieces without the need to use the tailstock.

One very important aspect of chucks is their ability to hold work very securely, and this varies to some extent according to the quality of manufacture. It is also vital for chucks of this kind to run absolutely true when screwed onto the lathe spindle, which some do. If a chuck is running even slightly out of true it will be a nuisance, and should be returned to the supplier, but there is always a possibility, especially with a secondhand lathe, that the lathe bearing is at fault.

A good chuck system will pay for itself, and then continue to work well for many years. The Multistar Duplex system shown here is likely to remain hard to beat for engineering quality and efficiency of operation.

It can be difficult for an experienced woodturner to comprehend the finer points of a chuck system when seeing it for the first time, so the problem is even greater for beginners. It may be possible to arrange for the supplier to demonstrate his product, if his works is not too far away, but the best approach is to go to a woodworking show and see the systems demonstrated there. Shows of this kind are inclined to be crowded, but towards the end of the day they slacken off, and this is the time to pick.

Fittings for Chuck Systems

The most important fitting for chuck systems is the chuck body itself, together with a retaining ring which screws onto the front. This can be purchased initially, together with one or more sets of jaws, and other units can be bought as the need arises.

Operating a Chuck System

The Multistar Duplex system has been used in my workshop for some time, to my entire satisfaction, and I will give some idea of its potential. It derives the Duplex part of its name from the fact that its sets of jaws can be made either to open when the retaining ring is tightened, or to close. This means that the jaws can open into a recess cut in a piece of timber, gripping from the inside, or they can close upon a piece of wood which is inserted into them. Whether they

Multistar chuck showing small diameter jaws.
These chucks are available with threads to fit most
popular lathes.

The Tommy bar, shown here, fits into hole in chuck
to steady it as the chuck is tightened with a special
spanner.

Chuck body shown fitted with large jaws, suitable
for turning bowls, plates, and similar items. When
the chuck is in expansion mode the jaws will
expand into a prepared recess in a workpiece as
the chuck is tightened. In compression mode they
will close, and can be used to grip a small stub
turned on the wood.

The Multistar screw chuck is extremely efficient,
and does not use ordinary woodscrews, as is
normally the case. The special screws provided
give a strong grip in the timber. The woodscrew
chuck is held inside the jaws of the main chuck.

open or close is decided by whether or not certain parts are put into the chuck body when the jaws are fitted, but in either mode they are extremely effective. These chuck jaws can be obtained in a range of sizes, so there is something suitable for most workpieces.

The jaw action on these chucks is superb, they move beautifully, and remain equally spaced as they do so, which is more than can be said for others I have tried. There is also a range of pin chucks in different sizes, which can be held in the collet jaws. A pin chuck is a cylinder of metal, with a flat milled on it, which is pushed into a hole drilled in a workpiece such as a pepper pot or even a bowl blank. The secret of its holding power is a small pin, or thin cylinder of metal, which is laid lengthwise on the flat por-

tion of the chuck before insertion into the wood. The idea is similar to that used in an inertia reel seat belt on a car, in that as the lathe starts, the pin jams the chuck tight in its hole.

The Multistar chuck body is equipped for indexing, which is the equal spacing of holes in a turning, as required in a wheel hub for the spokes. Indexing is also used when wood is to be fluted with a router, or when equal sections are required around a bowl to take a repeat carving pattern. In this case it is achieved by means of a number of equally spaced holes which are drilled in the chuck body, and an arm which is fixed to the lathe. The arm has a projection on its end which fits into the holes on the chuck, and there are twenty four of these. If the wood is marked or drilled when the pin is in every third one, there will be eight equal divisions, if in every eighth there will be three, as required when marking a milking stool top for positioning the legs, and so on.

Tools for Woodturning

When selecting tools for woodturning, it is not advisable to buy what the tool manufacturers refer to as 'sets', and which they insist on supplying in cardboard boxes. These are collections of tools put together quite arbitrarily, and they usually contain items which beginners do not need, and professionals don't want. There is in fact no such thing as a universally accepted set of tools for woodturning, and the best way is to seek advice from someone who understands the matter before spending money, some of which may well be wasted.

Large Woodturning Projects

For most home workers a lathe which will accept a piece of wood three feet in length will do very well, and it is worth noting that long lathe beds produce real problems, in that very long work is demanding for an experienced turner, and most frustrating for a novice. In almost every case a long project can be made in two or even three pieces, and jointed by making a projecting pin on one piece to fit into a hole in the other.

Provisions for the turning of large discs vary among makes, and on some lathes very large discs cannot be turned. One popular system is the rotating headstock design, as used on the Tyme lathes to good effect. The illustrations show this, and it is extremely simple. On most lathes the headstock is fixed permanently in one position, but on the Tyme it has a clamping lever underneath, and when this is slackened it can be rotated through ninety degrees so that the end of the spindle faces the turner, enabling large discs to be fitted.

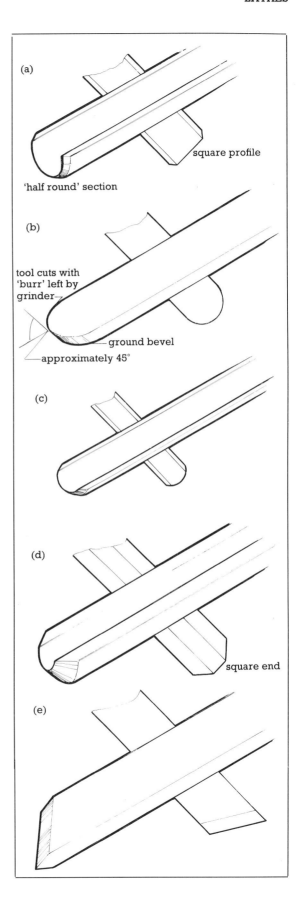

Woodturning tools: (a) Roughing gouge. (b) Round nosed scraper. (c) Spindle gouge. (d) Disc turning gouge often referred to as a 'bowl' gouge. (e) Skew chisel used for smoothing surfaces and for detail cutting, but hard to master without proper instructions.

COPYING ATTACHMENTS

The type of copying device described here is an attachment for a lathe, and should not be confused with automatic lathes or extremely expensive copiers, as used in high volume industrial production. The copying attachment shown in the illustrations is available for the MiniMax range of lathes, distributed in this country by Luna Tools & Machinery, who are based at Bletchley, Milton Keynes. The attachment is shown on a MiniMax T90 lathe, but with minor modifications it could probably be fitted to other makes.

Copying attachments of this kind are expensive, often costing as much as, or more than, the lathe itself, and they do have limitations of which the buyer should be aware. Their main advantage is in the production of long runs of certain shapes, as for example balusters for staircases, or legs and other turned parts for furniture. As with most other tools, some designs of copier are better than others, and the MiniMax is the best I have used. One reason for this is its heavy duty construction, which coupled with a high standard of engineering produces a very good performance. Another big point in its favour is that the cutter is well designed, having the shape and action of a gouge rather than of a scraper.

Construction

The copier itself consists of a stout cylindrical steel bar mounted in a heavy sheet steel frame. The cutter is mounted in a carrier which fits on the bar, and has a chain and sprocket drive by means of which it can be moved smoothly, parallel to the lathe bed. A flat bar is fitted at the front of the attachment, to which the item to be copied can be secured. This may be a flat template, or a turned pattern. The copying process relies upon a steel pin which rides against the template or pattern, and which is spring loaded. As the pin moves along the template it follows the profile, and its movements are duplicated exactly by the cutter.

Woodturners use a variety of tools, of different shapes, whereas the copier has only the one gouge-like cutter. Fine details, such as beads or V cuts, are therefore beyond its capabilities,

but this is not really much of a drawback – one simply leaves a flat surface where such detail is required, and puts it in by hand when the main copying is completed. This is simplified by the provision of a small toolrest on the copier, which is hinged, and can be swung into position when needed.

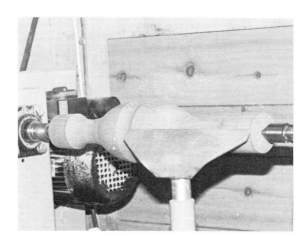

The T120, like all MiniMax products, runs quietly, and will handle heavy or awkward workpieces with ease.

Close up of tool carrier on copier, showing the gouge shaped tool. This is sharpened by means of a small oilstone, but only on its inside bevel. The outside must not be touched. The small black metal square behind the perspex guard is hinged, and when the guard is pivoted away the black section can be swung down to act as a toolrest for freehand insertion of final details.

Operation

A copier of this kind, once set up correctly, can be used effectively by a completely unskilled person, since the process consists of moving the cutter along the work by means of the handle, lowering the cutter a fraction by turning a knob, then repeating this procedure until the wood has been cut sufficiently for the pin to ride the full length of the pattern. No further cutting is then possible without altering the setting of the copier.

It should be noted that the design of these devices is such that the cutter must always work at ninety degrees to the axis of the workpiece, and that cutting will occur both 'uphill' and 'downhill'. This happens with every make of machine and does mean that surface finishes such as are produced by skilled freehand turners cannot be obtained. The finish on good quality hardwood will, however, be quite reasonable, and can be cleaned up with abrasive paper if desired. Where large numbers of similar items are required – for example in mass production – the copying is normally done by a semi-skilled worker, the resulting pieces being left at a little more than the desired finished diameter, so that they can quickly be skimmed by a turner with a sharp gouge, and polished. This will take a skilled operator little time, since all measuring and shaping has been done, and it is only necessary for a fine shaving to be removed.

Further Attachments

Long work between centres always presents problems in woodturning, and where much of

Close shot of copier, showing the small adjustable metal bar, to the right of the lower handle bar, which steadies the template against the spring pressure of the copier pin.

this kind of copying is envisaged it is worthwhile to invest in one or perhaps two lathe steadies. These are available for the MiniMax in a design which does not interfere with the free passage of the cutter, and if correctly set such steadies will greatly reduce the aggravating vibration which can result from the elasticity of the timber.

The guide pins of these machines bear quite heavily against the template, which should therefore be made from a material which will withstand the resulting wear. For very long runs the best choice will be metal, but thick plastic sheet, or hardwood a quarter to three eighths of an inch in thickness can be used. A smear of grease along the edge of the template also helps.

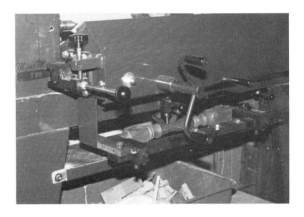

Copier fitted to T90 lathe with a turned pattern locked in position.

Copiers of this kind have not yet achieved the popularity they deserve in this country, but they are widely used on the Continent, and are well worth considering where repetition work is called for. If possible it will be advisable to arrange for a demonstration by the distributor at his premises, or to see a copier in use at a woodworking show. The weight and size of such machines should also be considered, since in my view it would be dangerous, if not impossible, for some of them to be fitted to or removed from a lathe single handed.

Those who wish to follow up the idea of woodturning might like to read another book of mine, *Modern Woodturning*, also published by Bell & Hyman, and perhaps to telephone 0225 22617 for full details of two and three day woodturning courses.

13
THE GRINDER

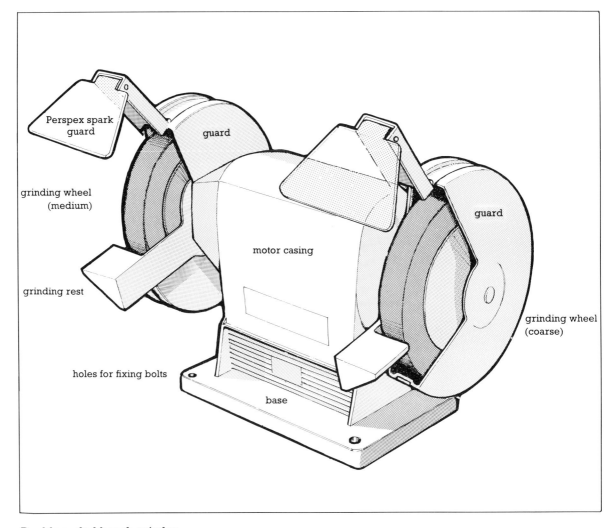

Perspex spark guard

guard

grinding wheel (medium)

grinding rest

motor casing

guard

grinding wheel (coarse)

holes for fixing bolts

base

Double ended bench grinder.

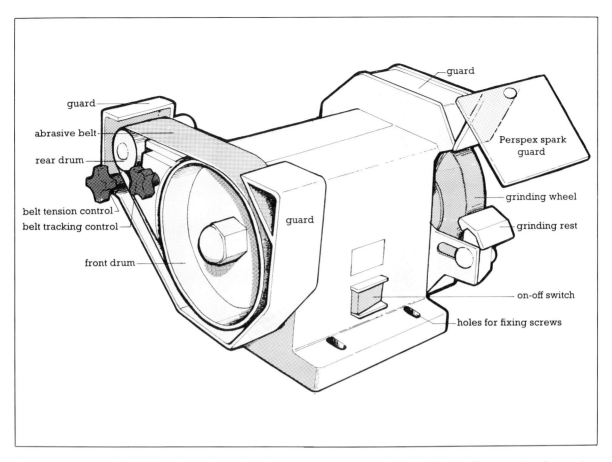

A combined grinder/linisher from Elu, which has become very popular. It is fitted with normal carborundum wheel at right, and flexible abrasive belt at left.

Grinding machines are not woodworking tools, but they deserve some mention here because they have their uses in keeping various cutters and tools in shape. Those machines sold for general home workshop use are normally fitted with carborundum wheels, which are grey in colour, and it is customary for manufacturers to fit a coarser wheel on the left hand spindle, this being intended for relatively rapid removal of metal. The wheel on the right will be of a finer grade, and is used for sharpening and finish grinding. The machine itself is very simple, being a motor housed in a suitable case, with a base which can be screwed to a bench or stand, and having a spindle protruding from each end for the fitting of abrasive wheels.

Most grinders of this kind are double ended, since very little extra cost is involved in making provision for the extra wheel. In some cases, however, the spindle on the left may be provided with a wire brush or a polishing mop, rather than a grindstone.

Construction

Grinding wheels in many types of carborundum, aloxite, silicon carbide, and mixtures of the last two, are available for fitting to these tools, but in the main they will not concern the woodworker, who can usually manage for the general run of workshop operations with the stones which are fitted to the machine when it is made. The same comment applies with regard to the grade of the wheels, or the question of how coarse or fine they are. Fine stones have a high grit number, coarse stones a low one, since the number refers to the number of holes in a square inch of mesh through which the granules have passed.

If the guard is removed from a wheel there will be found to be a thick paper washer on each side of the stone, centrally positioned. These washers carry printed information about the type and grade of the wheel, and they must not be removed, since they provide a cushioning effect when the retaining nut is tightened. If they are removed there is danger of the wheel breaking up at some stage. It is also important to avoid overtightening the retaining nuts and pinching the wheel. These nuts should be pulled up gently with a spanner, without any force.

Use

It is often suggested in grinder advertising that such items as planer knives, plane irons from hand planes, twist drills, and cutters used in spindle moulder blocks, can be sharpened on these machines quite easily. This is not in fact true, unless the person reading the advertisement has been fully trained in such operations. Items such as I have mentioned are now far from cheap, and they can be ruined in seconds by improper application to grinders, so it is far better to send them away to be restored when they are worn or damaged.

This eight inch (wheel diameter) Wolf double ended grinder has been in regular service in my workshops for fifteen years. It can be bench mounted, or as here fixed to a purpose-made metal pedestal. This is a high quality tool, and very cheap grinders should be avoided. They have low quality bearings, and are extremely noisy.

In general terms it is fair to say that tiny grinders with wheels under six inches in diameter are virtually useless, and unless to be used on extremely rare occasions for operations of little consequence, they are best avoided. Double ended grinders with six or seven inch wheels are far better, though very much dearer. They run almost silently if they are from a good maker, unlike the five inch versions which in most cases make fiendish noises, because the motors, and the bearings in which the spindles run, are of very poor quality. Eight to ten inch grinders are excellent for those who can afford them, and will withstand running all day for years on end. This degree of excellence is of course reflected in the price. It is worth noting that the price differential in the case of six and seven inch machines is slight, this being due to the fact that the machine is the same in both cases, the only difference being the size of the wheels. I have been using a Wolf eight inch machine for some fifteen years, and it runs all day when I am woodturning. It is still in good health, although its wheels have worn down a fair way.

Safety

Metal guards are provided, and these surround as much of the wheels as is practical. The flimsy plastic sheets which are hinged to the guards are spark deflectors, and would be of little help if a wheel broke up while in use. They should be interposed between the worker's eyes and the wheels, although many people do not like them because it is extremely difficult to keep them dust free in a woodworking environment. This is because they are in an electromagnetic field, and being made of plastic material they build up static charges, which attract dust. One must either become accustomed to the constant need to wipe them clean, or use a pair of high impact goggles instead. Under no circumstances should grinders be operated without eye protection of some kind.

14
UNIVERSALS

It is generally accepted that machines which have been designed for one specific purpose are more efficient than the universal or combination tool, which is designed to be capable of a number of woodworking operations, and in which some element of compromise is inevitable. Considerable progress has, however, been made over the past twenty years or so in the design and construction of multipurpose woodworking machines, some of which are now worthy of careful consideration.

Really first class machines of this variety are necessarily expensive, and this must be borne in mind, but it is advisable to resist any temptation to purchase cheap versions, no matter how attractive they may appear from advertisements, or when viewed in a showroom. It is not possible to manufacture a cheap universal machine without cutting corners in quality of materials and production methods, and this sort of thing can produce machines which are a constant source of irritation because they produce inaccurate work in spite of careful setting, and they may even be dangerous.

There are various approaches to the question of providing machinery which can operate from a single power source to provide facilities for a number of different woodworking operations, and this is at times very confusing to anyone new to such systems. This section of the book therefore explains these approaches in a manner which will assist a beginner in selecting a universal or composite machine which will satisfy his or her specific requirements. The machines which are brought together in this way are set and operated in basically the same man-

ner as are individual machines, so operating procedures can be found in the relevant chapters. Here we need to look at the ways in which machines are combined in order to save space and capital.

The labels applied to composite machines seem to be interpreted in slightly different ways by those who use them, and indeed by manufacturers, which leads to confusion. The basic types of machine combination are fortunately fairly clear cut, but there will always be some designs which do not quite fit exactly into any category.

The Universal Machine

In my own view, after having tested many kinds of combination machine over the years, the best approach is the universal machine, normally consisting of circular saw, planer thicknesser, mortiser, and spindle moulder, all housed in one unit, and driven by one motor of suitable type and power. In this category the MiniMax C30 is a good example, taking up little more than a square yard of floor space, incorporating excellent design and construction, and being priced within the range of the serious home woodworker. It has heavy steel tables, and performs very well, but one of its most appealing features is the system used to change the drive from one unit to another, which is done by sliding a control bar to align a small symbol with a mark, twisting the control bar to engage the selected machine, and moving a small lever to lock the setting. Changeover from one setting to another is literally a matter of seconds, and one does not even see the drive belts.

The Composite Machine

An alternative to this is the composite machine, which consists of a number of individual machines mounted on a table around a central power source. This idea also works quite well, and has the advantage for a beginner of enabling the system to be built up piecemeal as funds allow. The motor and circular saw could be purchased first, followed perhaps by the planer thicknesser, mortiser, and spindle moulder. Most designs of this nature seem to have cast alloy tables on the machines, which is something I would prefer to avoid, but they do work quite well.

Other Types of Machine

There is also a wide variety of machines which are basically a lathe, circular saw, or planer thicknesser, to which attachments can be fitted. This type of tool can look extremely attractive when operated by a professional demonstrator, who can change attachments in a matter of seconds, but it might be as well to insist on fitting one or two attachments yourself before actually purchasing. It is also worth remembering that the work will need to be planned carefully, so that all operations are completed without the need to refit an attachment which has already been used and removed.

Cost is an important factor for most of us, and after a thorough study of this book it may be that many people will decide that a good bandsaw, a planer thicknesser with mortising attachment, and a radial arm saw, would serve their purposes adequately.

De Walt dust extractor connected to MiniMax C30 universal for efficient chip removal during surface planing operations.

A well designed universal machine from Startrite. This kind of machinery is excellent for those with space problems, or as a back up tool in small businesses. Independent machines are generally preferable, if space and cash will permit their installation.

THE SPINDLE MOULDER

In general terms it is fair to say that spindle moulders are large examples of the sort of machine which is produced when a router is used inverted in a table, and it is likely that anyone accustomed to using a router in this way would take to a spindle moulder fairly easily. The spindle, as the machine is normally called, is capable of doing pretty well the same things as the inverted router, but on a larger scale. It is only fair to point out that misuse or abuse of these tools can result in workpieces being kicked back or rejected by the cutters in a very alarming manner. Well designed and constructed spindle moulders are not inherently dangerous, but unfortunately many people who use them are, and this has given the machine a bad

Spindle moulder block set up in MiniMax C30 universal woodworking machine. Note spare collars and cutters in box. Tooling like this is initially expensive, but well worth its cost.

name. The situation is exacerbated by the fact that some of the lightweight spindle moulders now available for home or hobby use are not well designed or constructed.

Construction

The illustrations show the spindle moulder which forms part of the MiniMax C30 universal machine, and the guard assembly, which carries the fences, is the standard version. For serious spindle work this would require either modification, or replacement by a more sophisticated type, the main shortcoming of the standard assembly being the fact that the fences are not individually adjustable. The significance of this will be revealed as we examine the machine in detail.

Spindle moulders take their name from the vertical spindle, which can be raised or lowered relative to the table, usually by means of a handwheel. The spindle is designed to carry a finely balanced steel cutter block, into which a variety of knives can be fitted for specific operations. Some models, such as the one shown here, also have provision for the fitting of a small collet chuck to the top of the spindle, which will accept router cutters. This is a somewhat pointless idea in practice, since the secret of success with all cutters is adequate tip speed, and this is simply not available because of the small diameter of the router cutters. Results of a sort can be achieved, but only with fine cuts and slow feed.

The cutter block supplied with or purchased for the spindle moulder will normally be about four or five inches in diameter, and is slotted to accept the knives. The overall effective diameter of the block plus cutter projection gives tip speeds which are very high, and if the knives are sharp, good finishes can be obtained, even when cutting across the grain. The workpiece MUST, as always, be fed into the rotation of the cutters, never in the same direction. Springs, either bought for the purpose or home-made from timber, should be used wherever possible to hold wood firmly against both fence and table as it is machined, and hands should never be allowed near or to the rear of the cutters. Timber being machined should first have been prepared, so that it is flat and will ride safely against table and fence with full support. If this is not observed there may be a slight twisting of the workpiece at some point during the operation, which can result in a severe kick back.

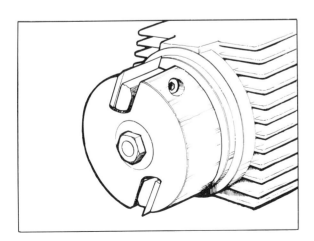

A rebating block in place on a De Walt motor spindle.

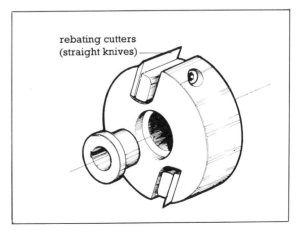

rebating cutters
(straight knives)

Components of a De Walt moulding block.

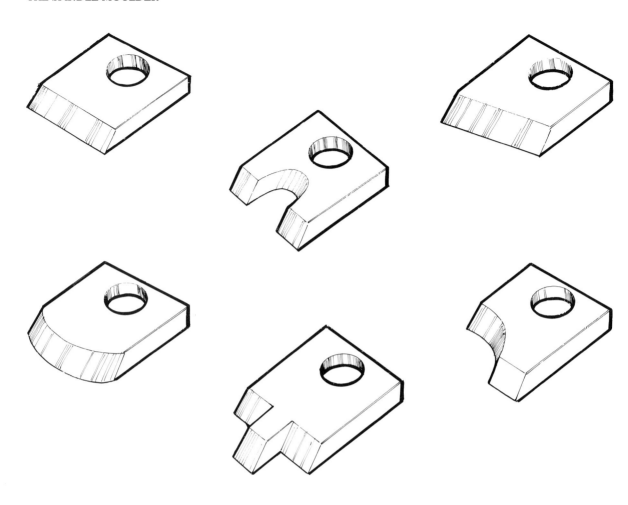

Some common cutter shapes for the spindle moulder. The hole in the cutter fits over the peg in the block for safety.

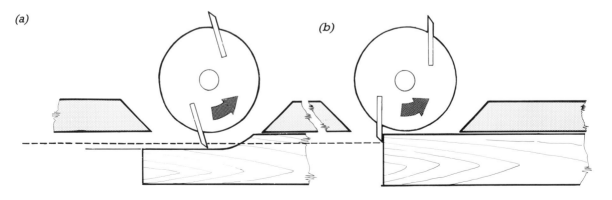

(a)

(b)

Cutter is at full depth when tip and centre of block are in line at 90° to surface.

Checking depth of cut as at (b) will give a false result.

The guard assembly carries the fences, and is often equipped with an attachment point for a dust extractor hose, and on the more sophisticated versions the fences are capable of backward or forward adjustment by means of fine screw feeds. If the fences cannot be adjusted in this way, care must be taken to see that support is provided by the take off fence when the edges of timber are being completely moulded. If part of the original edge is being left untouched, the width of the workpiece is unchanged, and it will receive support from the take off fence. If all the edge is moulded, however, this will not be so, and accidents have occurred through lack of understanding of this point.

Types of Moulding Block

The moulding block which can carry pairs of cutters is the most commonly used, a wide variety of cutter shapes being available, plus pairs of blank cutters which can be ground to shape by the user to suit the requirements of a special job. There are also 'solid profile' moulding heads, designed specifically for one job, with the cutters as an integral part of the head. These are expensive, and used mainly in industry on long production runs. A third type was in use for many years, but is now not commonly found, having been banned in many countries on safety grounds. This is the French head, and there is no moulding block as such. The cutters are flat steel bars which are positioned in a vertical slot in the actual spindle of the machine, each end of the bar being profiled.

Operation

The moulding block with a range of cutter shapes is therefore of most interest to woodworkers in general, and the performance of this device will depend upon the sharpness of the

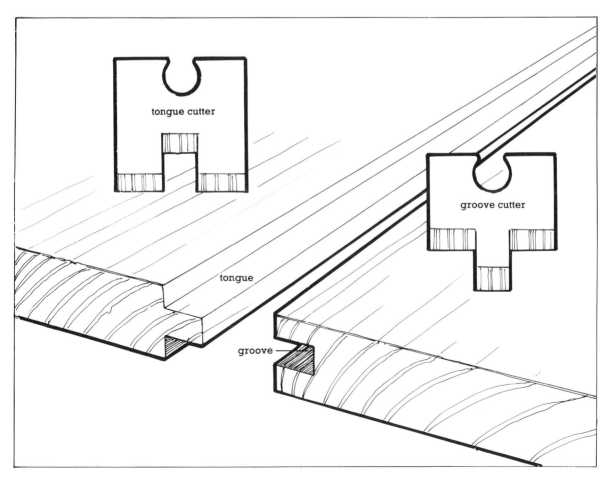

Tongued and grooved edges can be produced easily with the appropriate cutters in a moulding block.

cutters, and the accuracy with which they have been fitted into the block. Ideally the projection of the two cutters from the block should be exactly equal, so that they do the same amount of work. In this respect they are similar to planer knives, in that if one cutter projects more than the other it will do all the work, and the effective cutting speed of the tool is halved. In practice, if one cutter projects slightly more than the other, but both are sharp and the feed rate of the material to them is slow, the results will be fairly good.

When moulding or rebating is required on the edges of straight workpieces, they are fed into the cutters along the front fence, and supported by the rear one after passing the knives. Curved edges are moulded with the aid of a ring fence, or bearing ring, positioned above the cutter block, just as an overhead roller bearing is used for this purpose with a router inverted in a table. As previously stated, a router used in this way is effectively a small spindle moulder, and for this reason it will provide valuable experience for those who need to progress to spindle moulders.

Dedicated spindle moulders are expensive, and home users will normally either be quite well able to manage without one, or would be best advised to cope with their moulding re-quirements by other means, such as the use of a moulding block in a sawbench or as an attachment to a radial arm saw.

Safety

Most spindle moulder accidents arise from workpieces being allowed to move fractionally WITH the direction of cutters at some stage, whereupon tremendous forces are generated by the cutters, and in some cases hands have been dragged into contact with them. As with other machines, some operations are more difficult to carry out safely than others, and the beginner may not be aware of this. If it is really considered necessary to install a machine of this kind, a few days instruction from a competent and experienced instructor will be worth every penny. It must also be noted that operations with woodworking machines which involve a workpiece which is fully supported by table and fence being fed to a cutter or cutters are reasonably straightforward. Some work with spindle moulders, however, involves 'dropping on', or starting a cut partway along a workpiece by swinging it into the rotating cutters. Such situations do present considerable danger when an inexperienced operator is involved, and if they are attempted there must be no attempt to take heavy cuts.

15
THE POWERED FRETSAW

The first woodworking machine I ever owned was a treadle driven fretsaw, presented to me by my father when I was about fourteen years of age, and I have retained an affection for saws of this kind. The modern electrically driven tools are a lot easier on the leg muscles, and considerably more efficient. The model described here is the best of several I have tried, and is in regular use in my workshop.

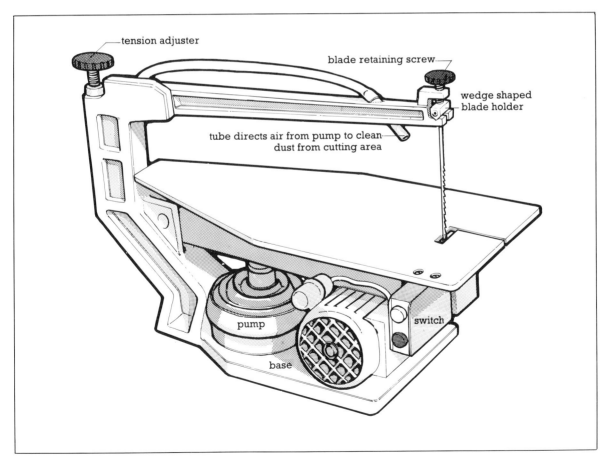

The Hegner fretsaw – robust, quiet, and extremely efficient.

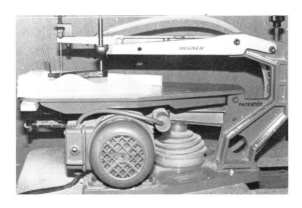

The Hegner powered fretsaw is the finest example of this type of machine I have yet seen. The air pump, which clears dust away from the marked line which is being followed, can be seen beneath the lower arm. The hold-down device, attached to the upper arm, is very effective indeed, but not supplied as standard.

A three legged stand is a useful accessory for the Hegner fretsaw.

Construction

A powered fretsaw is basically similar to the hand held version, in that a fine blade is held under tension in a frame, and has a reciprocal action, cutting on its downward strokes only. Hand fretsawing, other than for very small pieces, is a long and somewhat tedious business, particularly in fairly thick wood. The powered machine speeds up the process considerably, and removes the drudgery from the job.

The Hegner machine shown here has been demonstrated at the main woodworking shows for many years now by my friend Frank Scofield, who is an acknowledged expert with the tool. Some of his work, which is displayed at these shows, is of a quality which is almost unbelievable, as is his dexterity with the saw, and there is always a crowd around his stand. Most of us may not have the time to acquire anything like this expertise, but Frank reveals just what the machine is capable of, and although not cheap the Hegner is a valuable addition to almost any workshop.

There are several sizes of saw in the Hegner range, and the intending purchaser should consider his or her specific intentions, since the main limitation of powered fretsaws is obviously the distance between the blade and the column at the rear of the table. Most jobs done on these machines tend to be in relatively thin wood, plastic, or perhaps metal, using the appropriate blade type from the large range available. It should be observed, however, that this machine will cut hardwoods or softwoods up to two inches thick with considerable efficiency.

One of the annoying aspects of working with hand fretsaws, and with some powered versions, is the constant need to blow the sawdust away from the marked line which is being followed. The Hegner takes care of this automatically, using a concertina type pump, somewhat reminiscent of an aneroid barometer, which is situated below the table. This feeds a stream of air through a tube to a point above the cut, and keeps the markings free from obstruction.

A recent improvement to what was already a very good machine is the introduction of a speed control unit, which enables infinite speed variation between top speed and zero. This unit can be purchased and fitted by existing owners, and will enhance the versatility of the tool. It also permits lower speeds to be used when cutting materials other than wood, which is sometimes very desirable.

Operation

The cutting action of this type of saw tends to pull the wood towards the table, since the blade cuts on the downstroke, but newcomers to the machine frequently find difficulty in controlling the work because the blade will try to lift the wood as it moves upwards. Overcoming this is a matter of practice—the feed of the timber

must always be forward and down to the table, rather than merely a forward movement as with a bandsaw, and the blade must be permitted to cut, rather than forced to do so.

Some powered fretsaws are very sensitive to blade tension, but the Hegner is more tolerant in respect of this. Basically, if the blade is heavily overtensioned it is likely to break, and if too little tension is applied other problems can appear, such as the blade bowing in the cut. As with bandsaws, there is really no accurate system of judging this, and I have found that with a good machine it is best to err on the side of

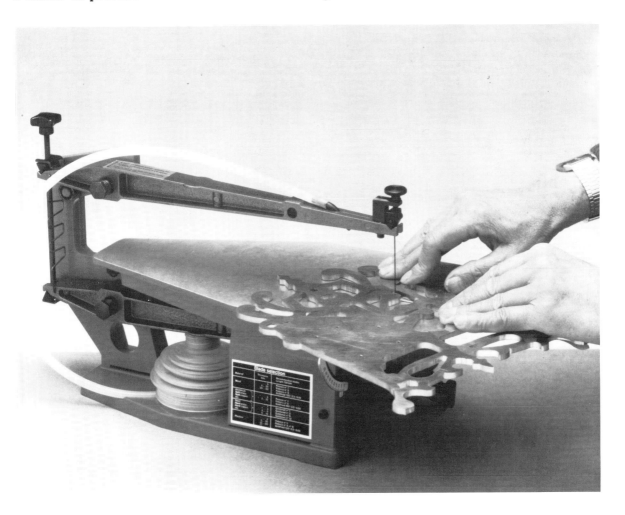

The fretsaw is ideal for intricate jobs such as clock making, giving a clean cut and even finish.

slight over tensioning. The tension control knob of the Hegner is at the rear of the upper arm, and the blade tension should be fully released when the machine is to be unused for a time. Applying tension is a simple matter of turning the control clockwise, and users soon get the feel of the job.

Attachments

The larger versions of the Hegner machine can be fitted with a hold down attachment, which can be attached by means of two Allen screws. This carries a flat metal plate or shoe at its forward end, which has provision for vertical adjustment. The operator adjusts the shoe so that it just touches the workpiece, and the device works well. A thin vertical rod is also incorporated to act as a guard.

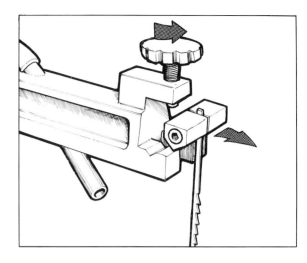

The simple and efficient blade mounting system on the Hegner saw. Blades can be changed very quickly.

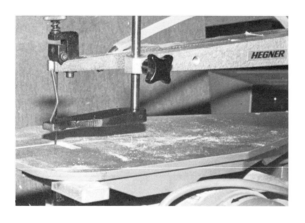

The hold-down device can be positioned by releasing the retaining screw and moving the shoe up or down. The small cranked steel rod acts as a guard. Note that the upper blade retaining screw has been slackened, ready for the removal of the blade.

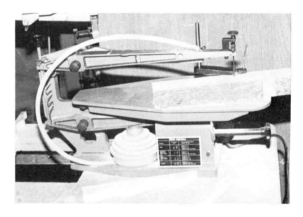

The blade tensioning knob is at the rear of the upper arm, and the tension should be released when the machine is not in use. These saws break surprisingly few blades, and work well on both hard and soft timbers up to two inches in thickness.

The Hegner saws run very quietly, and with little vibration, and their versatility has recently been increased by the introduction of a speed control device, which does not decrease the power. The on-off switch can be seen bottom right, and the control protruding below the table is the clamp lever for the table tilting mechanism. Note that the fitting of blades to their holding blocks would be a fiddly and awkward business without the specially shaped socket attached to the table into which the holding blocks can be fitted.

Blades

The full name of the machine shown is the Hegner Multicut, and one of the reasons for the long blade life which it normally provides, apart from its high standard of engineering, is the way in which the blades are gripped and held in the correct position relative to the table. This system is extremely good, as it not only gives long blade life, but also enables blade changing or replacement to be carried out in a remarkably simple manner, and in a very short time. This is due to the fact that the blade is not fitted directly to the arms, but first has a specially designed clamping block fixed at each end. The fitting of these is very easy, and spare clamping blocks can be obtained, enabling blades of different types and sizes to be kept to hand ready for instant changeover, with their own blocks in place.

Blade selection in respect of work to be performed is important with all saws, and the powered fretsaw is no exception. Even if blades intended for cutting metal or plastic are disregarded, there is still a good choice for the woodworker. It should be fairly obvious that the very fine blades will be used for fine work, having a large number of teeth, and being capable of producing very smooth sawn surfaces. Naturally a blade of this kind will not cut fast, and if this is the requirement, especially on thicker timbers, the stouter blades with less teeth and large gullets will be the wise choice. Quite heavy tension can be applied to these coarse blades, but some restraint is advisable in tensioning the fine ones.

Uses of the Fretsaw

A useful advantage which is offered by fretsaws is that where internal cutting is required, a starting hole can be drilled in the workpiece at a convenient point in the waste area, and the blade can be threaded through this, then clamped in the machine. When the internal cutting is completed, the blade is removed from the workpiece by reversing the original procedure. The table of the Hegner Multicut can also be tilted for angle cutting by using a simple mechanism, a facility which can be useful on some work.

Once confidence has been built up, it is possible to take the blades of these saws through quite remarkably tight curves, and the finer blades can turn a virtual ninety degree corner, so there are many uses for equipment of this type. Dust protection in the form of a mask, or some type of dust extractor, is a good idea just as with other saws, and the dust produced by fretsaws is particularly fine.

The superbly designed blade mounting system on these Hegner saws means that blades can be changed or replaced in a very short time. The blades are gripped at each end in a wedge shaped holder, and the upper one has been lifted clear in this picture. The lower one is removed from the lower arm by moving a spring clip.

16
THE FLAT DOWEL
JOINTER

One of the few real examples of a step forward in the woodworking machinery field in recent years has been the Elu flat dowel jointer. I am not often impressed by announcements of revolutionary machines, or alleged great strides in design or technology, since what are hailed as new ideas or new machines frequently turn out to be a rehash of something else. My reaction to the announcement of what was then called a 'biscuit jointer' was not, therefore one of exhilaration, and it was some time before I had an opportunity to try the tool.

It is my view that anyone familiar with normal jointing methods, such as the use of dowels, would be impressed after a fair trial of this device, which I now use constantly in carcase construction, the making of boxes, and almost any operation where boards have to be joined. I find it invaluable for edge jointing boards which are to form the tops of small tables and stools, for which I turn legs and rails, and for the quick, accurate, and simple slotting of drawer sides to accept the bottom. Since I always work alone I find difficulty in manhandling large plywood sheets on a sawbench, and use the flat dowel jointer to cut them to approximate size before trimming on a bigger machine.

Construction

The principle is simple, and very little practice will be required on odd bits of scrap timber before first class work can be done. The tool consists of an electric motor in a casing driving a small plate saw with tungsten carbide teeth, this whole unit being hinged to a special sole plate, so that the main part of the jointer can be tilted forward to project the saw to a predetermined distance through the plate. Fine adjustment is provided for this, and a fence can be fitted so that the distance of the saw cut from the edge of the timber can be varied.

Operation

When placed on the wood and plunged, (tilted forward) the sawblade cuts a curved slot in the material which permits the insertion of a flat dowel, or biscuit, and these can be purchased in boxes containing a thousand dowels. There are three sizes, the two larger ones being generally more popular, and the dowels are shaped to fit into slots cut in matching pieces of timber. They are manufactured from very highly compressed beech which has been cut with the grain running diagonally, and they have the property of expanding when they absorb moisture. Since modern polyvinyl acetate adhesives set by the action of wood in drawing water from them, they are ideal for use with these dowels, which expand in their slots and provide joints of tremendous strength. Unfortunately the dowels will readily absorb moisture in a damp workshop, so this fact should be borne in mind, as they can be difficult to force into the slots once they have swollen.

The instructions provided by the makers are clear and concise, and should present no problems for the new owner, who will have success with the very first project if they are followed carefully. I have recently read some instructions for an imported machine of quite a different type, which stated that a certain job should be done by 'blowing with a hammer', but there is no such delightful phraseology with Elu. Translations from foreign languages can be amusing, but in some there is an element of danger, since an important safety point could easily be missed.

The first step is to mark the wood at the points where slots are to be cut, and to align these marks with register lines which are engraved on the base of the tool. A few words on the physical operation of the machine are needed,

however, since when cutting slots the tool is effectively 'dropping on', and if this is done carelessly there is a chance of a kick back, but this is unlikely to cause injury in view of the manner in which the tool is held. Provided that the sole plate is firmly in contact with the wood, and the rotating blade is fed into the work at a sensible speed, there will be no trouble.

Uses of the Machine

Apart from speed and ease of operation, there is one big disadvantage with these flat dowels,

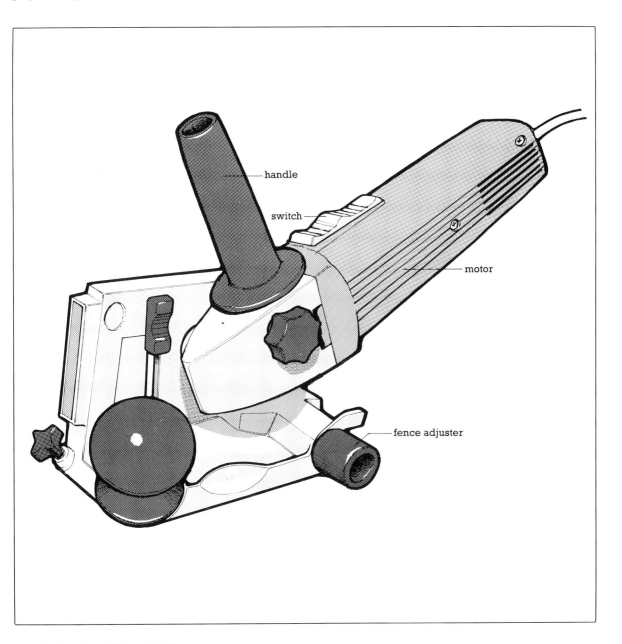

The Elu flat dowel 'biscuit' jointer.

129

which will be much appreciated by many users. This is that whereas round dowels must have their holes drilled in precise register in two directions, the flat variety is only subject to such precision in one. It will be seen that adjustment of the mated workpieces is possible in relation to the long axis of the dowels. A further point is that round dowels must be grooved to permit the escape of a glue when they are fitted, to avoid the hydraulic effect which might otherwise split the wood. This is not so with the flat type, since the shape of the groove permits the glue to exude at the ends.

Lateral precision in cutting the slots presents no problems because the fence works very well. It is designed so that it can be fitted with its guide in one of two positions, and most work will be done with the fence projecting below the surface of the sole plate so that it can be run against the workpiece. When it is necessary to cut slots distant from the edges of a job however, the fence can be inverted in the sole plate. This puts the lower edge of its guide level with the surface of the sole plate, so that it can run against a batten which has been fixed across the work.

Slotting and grooving can be performed with the machine, using it as a small circular saw, and I have found it an invaluable aid in toy-making, since it provides joints of great strength, which will withstand the rough treatment which youngsters frequently expect wooden toys to endure.

17
MISCELLANEOUS POWER TOOLS

THE ELECTRIC SCREWDRIVER

A well made electrically driven screwdriver is a magnificent tool for those who have large numbers of screws to drive, but is really of peripheral interest to the home worker, since it is expensive, and in most cases likely to be used only on odd occasions. Those who own an electric drill with speed control and reversing facility will be best advised to obtain an attachment for this, to enable the drill to be used as a screwdriver.

Electric screwdrivers from Wolf and Bosch. Both have variable torque, and can be reversed for the extraction of screws. Both are highly efficient in operation, but are too expensive for general home use.

Construction

The tool is often similar in appearance to an electric drill, since it is basically just a powerful, low geared motor, fitted into a plastic case, with on-off and reversing switches built into the handle. The motor drives a shaft, the end of which protrudes from the casing and is shaped to accept the screwdriver drive bit assemblies, which are located on the shaft by spring clips. There is no chuck, as would be present on an electric drill, therefore the tool cannot be used for purposes other than the driving or removal of screws.

Since it is essential that the correct sized driving bit be used for any given screw, it will be obvious that a range of sizes will be needed, and this adds to the overall cost. The part of the assembly which actually enters the screw slot and applies the torque to the screw is shaped very much like the end of a hand operated screwdriver, but it runs inside a metal sleeve, which is spring loaded, so that the driving bit itself is normally not visible.

Tools of this nature are fitted with torque controls, which enable a given amount of twisting action to be applied, but if any attempt is made to exceed this pre-set amount, the drive slips. The torque setting is achieved by inserting special springs into the drive, these being of different strengths, and colour coded for ease of identification. Abuse of powered screwdrivers, apart from the use of the wrong bit, or a badly misshapen one, includes the use of the wrong spring, and the instructions provided by the makers should be adhered to in this respect.

Safety

Powered screwdrivers have a reputation for being difficult to use, and quite likely to jump off a screw and skid into the wood, causing damage to the surface. This is an unfair criticism, since if the correct driving bit for the screw in use is employed, and the bit itself is kept in proper order, this sort of thing does not happen. When it does, it is almost invariably the fault of the user.

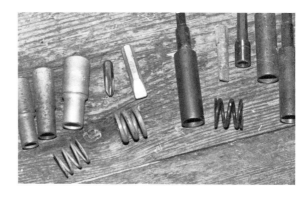

Range of driving bits, holders, and springs for Wolf and Bosch screwdrivers. The spring strength determines the torque loading, and the springs are colour coded.

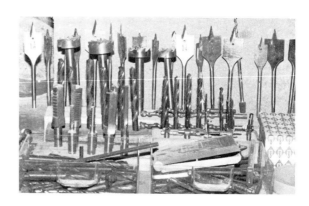

A selection of drill bits and router cutters can be built up over the years, but these items must be kept sharp.

BLOWERS

The powerful electrically driven portable blowers, which have been available for some years now, are in general underestimated by the home woodworking fraternity, although it is fair to say that their rightful place is fairly well down a sensible list of priorities.

Construction

These devices are really just fans mounted in special casings, with air intake and outlet ports to which nozzles or dust bags can be fitted. Their principal use is in cleaning down machines, and removing dust and chippings from crevices and corners. If in blowing mode, with the nozzle fitted to the outlet, and the dust bag not in use, they will direct a very powerful blast of air from the tapered rubber nozzle, but this can result in a minor dust storm in the average workshop, so they are normally used by giving gentle 'blips' of the switch, a process which works very well.

It is often useful, where no dedicated dust extraction system is installed, to be able to suck dust from machines, and this is particularly so in the case of bandsaws, which quickly produce masses of fine sawdust. If the blower nozzle is fitted to the air intake, and the dust bag to the outlet, the machine becomes a very efficient suction cleaner for this kind of work. The blower can also be used to force air in through the cooling slots on electric drills and motors, to remove any accumulated dust.

An electrically driven 'blower' as shown here is useful for cleaning down machinery. It produces a powerful blast of air, but is usually best used with little 'blips' of the switch. The rubber nozzle can be removed from the mounting shown here by twisting to the left. It is then repositioned on the bayonet mount at the centre of the fan cover, and a dust extraction bag is fitted at the outlet. This provides a powerful portable vacuum device, which is excellent for cleaning out bandsaw cases.

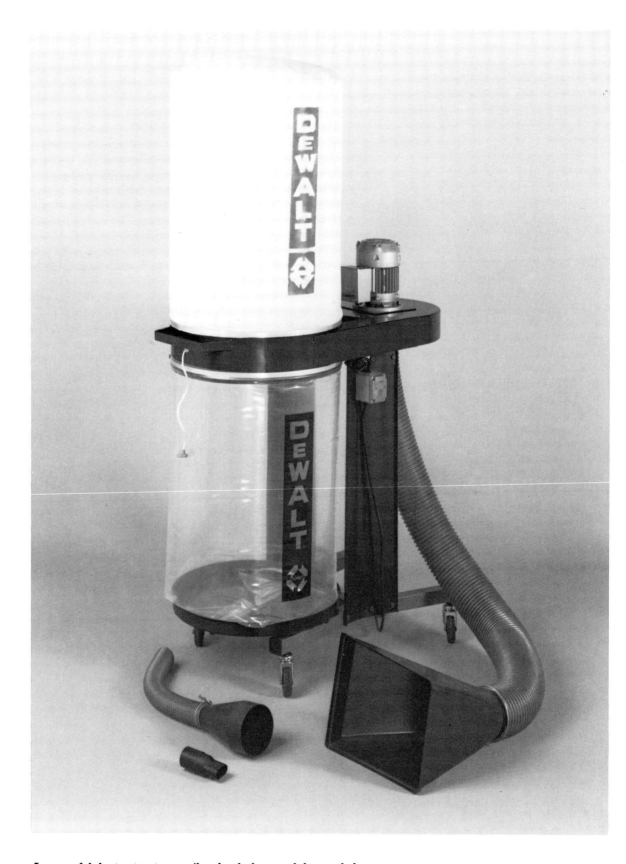

A powerful dust extractor, easily wheeled around the workshop.

18
WOODWORKING JOINTS

Woodworking joints must always be cut with great care, and the marking out of the workpieces must be exact. This is an enjoyable process when done with hand tools, but it can be very time-consuming. Good power tools provide both accuracy and speed of production, and where numerous identical joints have to be cut it is often only necessary to mark out the first one, the remainder being dealt with by positioning the wood against stop blocks clamped to the fence of the machine.

The Mortise and Tenon

The mortise and tenon joint is used widely in furniture construction, the procedure being to cut the mortises first, using a cutter of suitable size for the timber, and then to set a machine to produce tenons which are a good push fit in the mortises. In industrial production work, spindle moulders are used, fitted with special double cutters which will produce a finished tenon in one pass. Tooling of this kind is extremely expensive, however, and home workers are more likely to use some form of circular saw, either of the bench or radial arm variety.

If speed of production is a consideration, a dado head can be fitted. This removes a lot of wood in one pass, and so saves time, but an ordinary circular sawblade is commonly employed, and will do the job very well.

The pieces to be tenoned are first prepared to size for the job, and passed through a thicknesser to ensure that there is no variation what-

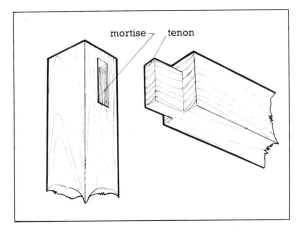

The tenon is narrower than the workpiece, the mortise is set in from the end of wood, so the tenon is hidden when the joint is assembled.

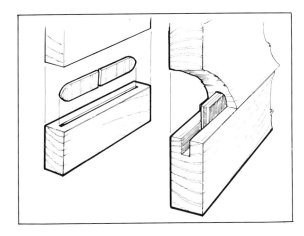

Splined joints can be 'through' or 'stopped' and are useful for edge jointing boards.

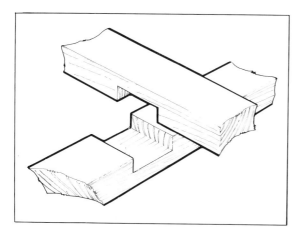

A cross halving joint. Test machine settings before starting on the actual work piece when making joints of any kind.

Half-Lap Joints

Half-lap joints are made in a similar manner, using overlapping cuts to provide the required width, but the depth setting is made so that when cuts are made into the wood from opposite sides, a few fibres remain as a 'web', connecting the timber across the centre, as shown on p. 140. This setting is tricky, but it will be found to be worth spending some time in getting it exactly right. If there are no connecting fibres, the cut is too deep, and if there are no gaps in the web it is too shallow. The process is really quite simple, and a little practice will soon produce good results.

When preparing timber to be used in a project which calls for joints of the kind described here, some extra timber should be prepared, and once a satisfactory joint has been made in this, the actual project can be dealt with.

soever in thickness among the workpieces, since any such variation would mean a corresponding variation in tenon thickness.

The depth of cut of the saw is now carefully set so that when a cut is made from each side at the extreme end of a workpiece, the resulting uncut portion will be of a thickness which exactly fits the mortise. This will be clear from the illustrations and the process is one of trial and error. When the depth of cut has been correctly established, a series of overlapping cuts can be employed to produce a snug fitting tenon of the required length.

Making Joints with a Bandsaw

Those who have a bandsaw which cuts accurately may prefer to cut some joints with it, using methods such as those shown in the sketches. These work well for tenons, and half-laps can be produced in a similar manner, using a series of cuts straight into the wood to remove the waste, and controlling the depth of cut by means of a stop block.

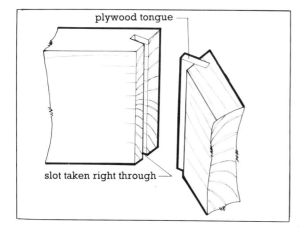

A normal splined mitre joint.

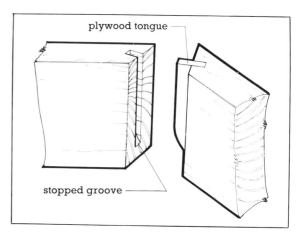

This splined mitre joint is 'stopped' so that the spline will not show at the front of the frame.

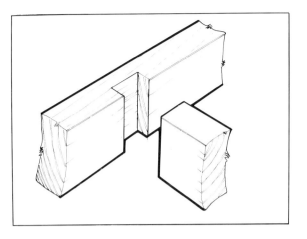

A notched joint, which is used in simple frame construction and is a form of housing.

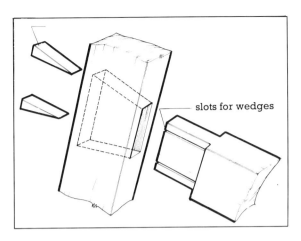

An exaggerated schematic view of 'fox wedged' tenon construction. Wedges are inserted in tenon slots before the joint is assembled. A joint of this kind cannot be taken apart.

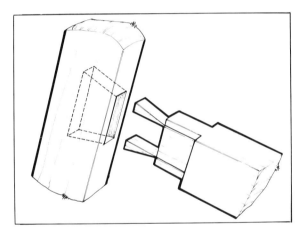

Wedges open the tenon as it is driven home, giving a very secure joint.

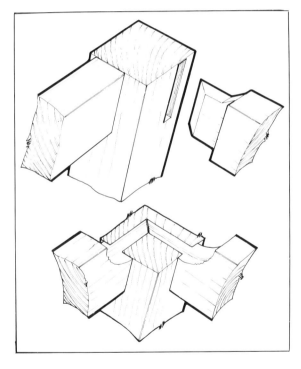

The construction of a mitred tenon joint for cabinet construction.

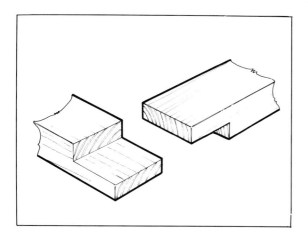

A standard form of half lap joint for simple frame corners.

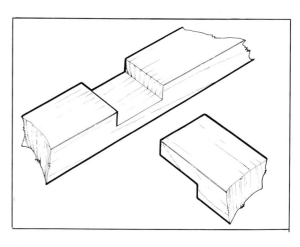

The bridle joint used in framing. This is very strong if carefully cut so that parts are a snug fit.

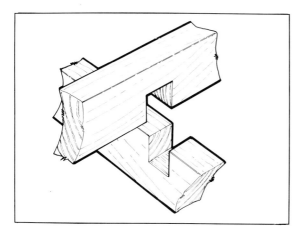

This notched joint is really a half lap with the timber on edge.

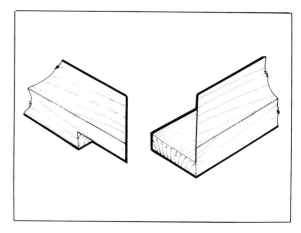

A mitred half lap. Completed assembly will show mitred corners on one side, half laps on reverse. Note that the mating pieces of wood are not identical.

A three-way lapped joint is complex and not often seen, but is an interesting exercise, requiring extreme accuracy in machine settings.

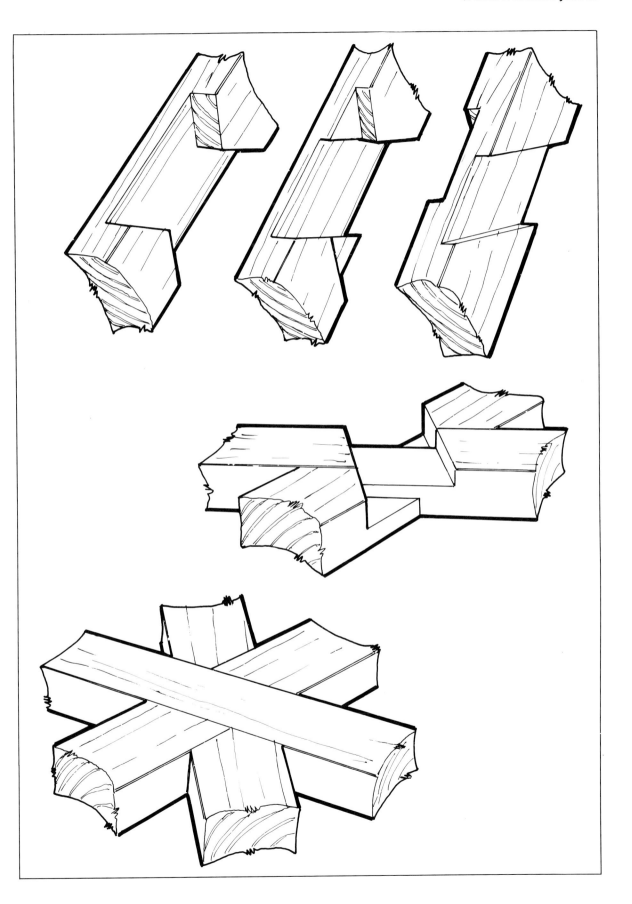

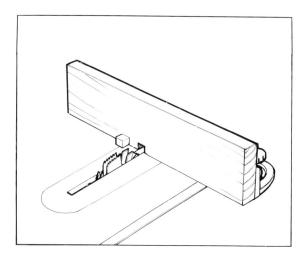

Saw table set up for box combing.

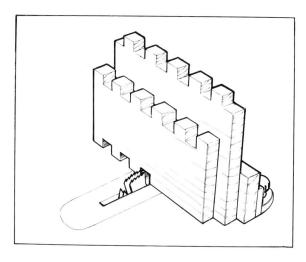

The pins on the ends of pieces are staggered to fit. As each cut is completed it is moved along to fit evenly into the spaces.

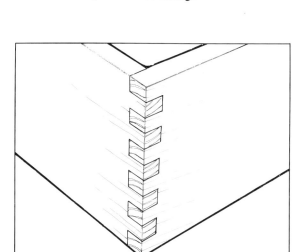

The completed joint must be a tight fit, and looks very attractive after sanding.

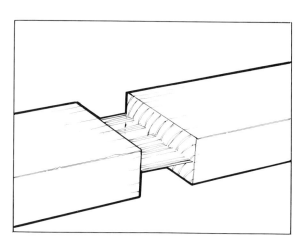

When setting a circlar saw or dado head for halving joints the depth of cut is set to leave a 'web' of fibres when cuts are made from opposite sides.

GLOSSARY

ARBOR: A shaft or spindle for mounting circular saw blades, sindle moulder blocks, etc.

BEVEL: A sloping surface joining opposite faces of a board, or of the blade of a cutting tool.

CHAIN & SPROCKET: A drive system often used for raising and lowering thicknesser tables. A chain runs round four toothed wheels or sprockets, enabling four screw threads to be operated by one handwheel.

CHAMFER: An angled surface joining adjacent faces of a board.

CHUCK: A device for holding workpieces on a lathe, or drill bits and cutters on a machine.

COLUMN: A vertical tubular part of pillar drill or radial arm saw.

COLLET CHUCK: As found on electric drills and routes, this contains small metal leaves or collets, which open or close as the outer casing of the chuck is rotated.

DADO: A trench cut with dado head, usually to house end of board, as in shelf construction.

DADO HEAD: A device consisting of two sawblades which can be separated by varying amounts as special chippers are interposed. Used for cutting dados.

DOWEL: A wooden peg for joining parts of wooden constructions. Sometimes flat 'biscuits' (see 'biscuit jointer').

DRILL, CONSUMER: The cheapest type of electric drill, intended for the occasional user.

DROPPING ON: This refers to the process of commencing a cut partway along a workpiece on a saw, planer, or spindle moulder.

FEED: The process of moving material forward into a cutter, or moving a portable machine forward to the workpiece.

FENCE: A device for guiding material being fed to machine, or for guiding hand held machine along a workpiece.

FENCE, MITRE: An adjustable fence used when crosscutting timber. Can be pre-set to produce a specific angle.

FENCE, RIP: One used to guide timber being cut lengthwise on circular saw. Can usually be tilted to permit ripping at angles other than ninety degrees.

HARDWOOD: These come from broad leaved or deciduous trees. Some softwoods are harder than many hardwoods, and vice versa.

JUDDER: The vibration set up between timber and rotating cutters, or between turning tool and rotating wood.

KNIVES: A term often used to mean blades, or cutters.

MILL FILE: A flat file used in saw sharpening, which has a rounded edge to facilitate working in the bottoms of gullets.

MORTISE: An aperture cut in a frame to receive the end of a rail which has been shaped to fit.

RIVING KNIFE: Often referred to as a 'splitter', this is a vertical metal plate behind a sawblade which prevents the wood from closing onto the rear teeth.

SPELCHING: The damage to the surface of a workpiece as cutter emerges which can normally be prevented by use of a spelch block or supporting piece of timber.

SAWBENCH: This is usually taken to mean a floor standing circular saw.

SCALE: A set of marks at measured intervals working in conjunction with a pointer to permit the accurate settings of machines.

SOFTWOOD: Softwoods come from coniferous trees, or from trees which do not shed their leaves.

STOP: An adjustable device to permit accurate settings on machinery, usually consisting of small metal blocks which can be adjusted to limit travel of cutters etc.

STOP BLOCK: A small wooden block clamped to a machine fence to permit repetition cutting, as when cutting numerous short pieces of equal length on radial arm saw.

TABLE: The table of a machine is a flat surface on which the material rides as it is passed over the cutters.

TABLE, SUB: A wooden table fixed to metal table of machine by the operator to protect the main table or to facilitate some specific operation.

TEMPLATE: A device having the characteristics of something which is to be copied, such as a shape to be cut out with a bandsaw or router, or an angle to be set between fence and table of a machine.

TENON: A shape produced on end of workpiece to enable it to be fitted into a mortise.

TENSION: The stretching force applied to blades of bandsaws or fretsaws.

TIP SPEED: The speed of saw teeth or edges of knives or cutters, usually measured in linear feet per minute.

WOBBLE SAW: A small circular saw blade which can be set to oscillate to various extents while rotating, so that it cuts a groove or trench.

INDEX

(Italicized numerals refer to captions or illustrations)

Abrasive paper 48, 93, 95, 99, 100, 113
Accidents *see* Safety
Adjustable stop 26, 57
Air pump 124, *124*
Allen key 46, 60, *85*, 126
Angled cuts 23, 25, 38, *41*
  on circular saw 48, *49*, *50*, 55
  on fretsaw 127
Angle setting
  on bench drill *20*
  on circ. saw 26
Anti-kick back fingers 49, *50*, *51*, 52, *73*, *74*, *75*, *76*
Auger *19*, 82, 86
Avon *106*

Backtracking
  on jigsaw 68
Baluster 108, 112
Bandsaw 8, 52, 54, 55–65, 92, 101, 118, 125, 133, 136
Banjo *see* Tool rest holder
Belt drive *79*, 96–7
Bench 108, 115
Bevel ripping 52
Bevelled mitre 48
Bits 12, 17, 18, *18*, *132*
  spade/flat bit 54
Black and Decker 89
  pad sanders *100*
  workmate *98*
Blades
  of bandsaw 55, *57*, 58, 59, 60, 61, 62
  blade jam 48, *64*, 65
  blade mounting system *126*, *127*
  blued steel blades 57, *57*, 61, 62, *63*, *65*
  carbon steel blade 27
  of circ. saw 23, *23*, 24, *24*, 26, 27, 28, 29, *29*, 30, 32, 35, 36, *41*
  combination blades 27, 36
  crosscut pattern blade 35, 36, 48
  of dowel jointer *129*
  of fretsaw 124, 126, *126*, 127, *127*
  of jigsaw 68, 69

making up your own bandsaw blade 63, *63*
  of planer 78
  of rad. arm saw 45, 47, *47*, 48, 49, 50, 52
  rip blade 36, 38
  silver blade 61, 62
  TCT blade 27, 35, 36, 38, 42, 71, 92, 128
Blowers 132–3, *133*
Bosch
  electric screwdriver *131*, *132*
Bowls 102, 110, *110*
Box 128
Box combing *140*
Bridle joint *138*

Carpenter's square *see* woodworker's square
Chamfer 91
Chip deflector 48, *73*, *75*, *76*
Chisel *17*, *19*, 82, 86
Chuck
  for bench drills 12, 16
  chuck key 16
  chuck system 109, *109*
  drill chuck 102, 104
  for lathe 107
  for rad. arm 54
  for router 87, 90
Circular saw 21–43, *21*, *22*, 130
  attachment to hand drill 14
  bench 135, *140*
  construction 23
  floor standing 21–38
  portable 38–43, *40*
  PS174 38, *38*, 39, *39*, 41, *41*, 42, *42*
  safety 10, 11, 13, 29
  TGS172 38, 42, *42*, *43*
Clamps 41, 48, 49
  for rad. arm saw 45
Clamping screw 31, 33, 45
Composite machine 118
Compound angles *41*, *43*
Compound bandsawing 65
Compound mitres 33

Copying attachment 112–13, *112*, *113*
Creep 33, 34, 35, 48
Crosscutting 41, 48, *49*, 53
  angled 41
  circ. saw 24, 25, 27, 31, *31*, 32, 38
  freehand 32
  with PS174 42
  rad. arm 10
Curve cutting 67, *68*
  on bandsaw *64*
  curved sanding 102, 103
  with fretsaw 127
  with router 92–3
  with spindle moulder 122
Curved shapes 58
Cutter 10, 17, 18, *18*, *29*, 78, *80*, 81, 82, 83, 84, 85, *85*
  cutter shank 12
  grinders 115, 116
  on lathe 112, 113
  speed 18
  spindle moulder *120*
Cutter block 53, 70, 73, 74, 75, 76, 77, 79, 119, 122
  guard 73
  router cutter 87, 88, *89*, 90, 91, 92, 93, 94, 119, *132*
Cut off work 42, *43*

Dado head *140*
  circ. saw 25, 30, 31, 35, 36
  rad. arm 46
De Walt
  dust extractor *118*
  rad. arm saw 44, *44*, 45, *45*, 46, 47, *48*, 49, *49*, 52, *53*, *54*
  router 71
  planer thicknesser 73, *74*, *75*, *76*, 82, *86*
  spindle moulder *119*
Depth of cut
  bandsaw 58
  circ. saw 24
  jigsaw 67, 69
  joints 136
  mortiser *84*, 86

portable planer 78, *79*
rad. arm 48, 54
Double ended grinder 115, *115*, 116
Dovetail joint 92
Dowel joint 128, 129
Drills and drilling techniques 12–20,
83, 86
attachments 54, 101, 102, *102*, *103*,
104, 131, 132, 133
bench drills 12, 14, *14*, 15, *15*, 16,
16, *18*, 86
consumer drill 12
drill stands 14
hand held drills 12, *13*
safety 13
speed controls 13
twist drills 116
Drive bit 132, *132*
Drive centre 107, 108, 117
Dropping on 128
Dust extractor 10, 18, 27, 52, 76, 77,
97, *118*, 121, 127, *134*
Dust extraction bag *98*, 100, *100*, 133,
133
Dust mask 27, 52, 97, 127

Edge moulding *92*, 93, *93*
Electrical hazards 9
Elevating handle 46, 48, 53, 54
Elu
circ. saw 38
flat dowel jointer 128, 129
grinder *115*
portable planer *78*
router *87*, 89, *90*, *92*, 93, *93*, *94*
sander *96*, *98*, *99*, 100

Faceplate 107
Fan 24, 133
Feeding material 10, 86, 125
Feed roller 73, 76
Feed table 70, 72, 78
Fence 25, 31, 32, 39, 42, 45, 69, 71, 72,
73, *76*, 78, *78*, *79*, *79*
dowel jointer 130
rad. arm *46*, 47, 48, 49, 52
router *87*, 90, 91, 93
spindle moulder 119, 121
Fibre 17, 101, 136, *140*
File
mill file 38
triangular 38
Flat dowel jointer 128–30, *129*
Flat work 102
Forstner bit 18, *20*
Frame for belt sander 98
Framing *138*
French head 121
Fretsaw 93, 123–7, *123*, *124*, 125, *126*,
127
Furniture leg 108, 112, 118
Furniture 135

Goblet 108
Grinders 63, 69, 114–16, *114*, *115*, *116*
grinding wheel 37
grindstone 115
Grooves 36, 45, 90, *121*, 130
Guard 8, 10
bandsaw *60*, 61, 63
circ. saw 26, *26*, 27, 29, *38*, 39, 40,

41, 42, *43*
guard assembly 121
planer thicknesser *76*
portable planer 78
rad. arm 44, 45, *47*, *48*, 49, 52, 53
router 71, 72
Guide *19*
Guide assembly 57, 58, 63
Guide pins 91, 113
Gullets 36, 38, 62, 27, 127

Handsaw 10, 32
Half lap joint 136, *138*
Handwheels 25, 76, 77, 119
Hardboard 48, 65
Hardwood 8, 24, 37, 46, 58, 71, 113,
124, *126*
Headstock 100–1, 106, *106*, 110
Hegner Multicut 93, *123*, *124*, 124,
126, *126*, 127, *127*
Height setting
on bandsaw 58
Hinges 93
Hold down device *124*, 126, *126*
Hosepipe 101, *103*
Housing joint 45, *51*, 91

In rip *47*, 49, *49*
Indexing 110–11
Industrial machines
planer/thicknesser 76
spindle moulder 135
Inverted router 93, *93*, 118, 122

Jacobs chuck *75*, 106
Jaw 109, 110, *110*
Jet clamps 85
Jig 16, *17*, 33, *33*, 34, *34*, 35, *35*, 78,
80, 84, 94, 100
for making blade 63, *63*, 68
Jigsaw 10, 66–9, *66*, *67*, 92
attachment to hand drill 14, 54
Joints 27, 36, 45, 135–40
butt joint 63
dowel joint 128
mortise and tenon *135*, *137*
scarfed joint 63
splined joint *136*

Kerf 27, 32, 37, 52, 62, *62*
Kick back 32, 45, 72, 119, 129
Knives 70, 71, 72, 73, 76, 77, 78
mortisers 83, *83*
planer 122
spindle moulder 119

Lathe *29*, 62, 101, 102, 105–13, *105*,
118
Lathe bed 106, 107, 111
Lathe steadies 113
Locating pin *17*
Locks 93
Locking lever 44
Locking nut 61
Locking screw 25, 28
Luna tools 112

Marked line cutting 68
Mill file 38
Minimax
C 30 Universal *55*, 58, *74*, *75*, *82*,

85, 113, 117, *118*, 119, *119*
T90 Lathe 112
T120 Lathe *107*, 108, *112*
Mitre cuts 33, *49*
compound mitres 33
Mitred half lap *138*
Mitring fence 48, 49, *49*, 63
Mitre guide 25, 26, 31, 32, *32*, 33, *33*,
35, 42, 58
Morse taper *106*, 107
Mortise *17*
joints 82, *83*, *85*, 93, 135–6, *135*
Mortisers 19, 65, 82–6, 101, 102, 117
attachments *19*, 73, *75*, 82, 82, 86,
86
chisel mortiser 82
handles 9
slot mortiser 82, *82*, 83, *83*, *84*, *85*
Mouldings 31, 91, 122
Moulding block 25, 31, *31*, *119*, 121,
121, 122
Moulding cutter 92
Moulding head 121
Mounting bar 28
Multistar Duplex 109, *109*, 110, *110*

Offcuts 32, 47
safety 9
Oilstone 37, 77, 78, *112*
Operator hazards 10
Outboard turning 106–7
Out rip *47*, 49, *49*
Overloading 24, 37, 38, 88, 98
Overload protection switch 49

Panel pin 47, 48
Pepper pot 110
Planers 54, 62, 70–81, 89
attachments 14
knives 116
pusher block *29*
safety 13
Planer/thicknessers 54, 70, 117, 118,
135
Plate 108, *110*
Polyvinyl acetate adhesive 118
Poppet barrel *see* tailstock
Portable planers 70, 78–81
Plywood 27, 47, 48, 65, 69, 92, 128
Pressure shoe 49
Pressure spring *50*
Protractor scale 25, 35
Push sticks 10, 28, *28*, 29, *43*, *51*, 52,
65, 72

Quill feed of bench drill 16

Radial arm saw 24, 39, 44–54, 89, 94,
94, 101, 102, *103*, 118, 122, 135
crosscutting 10
Ranging 37
Rebating 27, 30, *30*, 36, *51*, *54*, 70, 79,
81, 86, 91, *93*, 94, 122
block 119
Reciprocal cutting action 67, 68, 124
Removal of waste in cuts *59*, 65, *81*
Repetition crosscutting 48
Resawing 30, 52
Resin bonded materials 27, 36
Return spring *42*, *43*
Ring fence 122

Ring guard 53
Rip fence 25, 26, 28, 30, *31*, *33*, *40*, 42, *43*, 58
Rip scale 52
Ripping
    on bandsaw 58, 65
    on circ. saw 24, 27, 28, *28*, *29*, 30, 31, 32, 38, *40*, *43*
    on jigsaw 69
    on rad. arm 45, *47*, 49, 50, *51*, 52, 53
Rise and fall table 29, *30*
Riving knife 26, *26*, 27, *27*, 29, 42, *43*, 49, 52
Roller
    on planer thicknesser 73
Roller bearings 45
Roller take-off *30*
router 44, 62, 69, 87–94, *88*, 110
    attachments 53, 54, 94
    freehand routing *91*
    inverted router 118, 122

Sabre saw attachments 54
    see jigsaw
Safety 9–11, 27, 28, 63, 69, 71, 73, 89, 116, 121, 122, 129, 132
Safety return device *46*
Sanders 95–104
    belt sanders 95–8, *96*, *97*, *98*, 101
    bobbin sanders *53*, *102*, 103–4
    disc sanders 102–3, *102*, *103*
    drum sanders 102–3, *102*, *103*
    flap sanders *103*, 104
    freehand sanding 98
    orbital sanders 98–100, *99*, *100*, 101
    pad/palm sanders 100, *100*, 102
    sanding attachments 12, 14, 19, *20*, *50*, 52, *54*, 62, 69, 101–4
    sanding mask 19
Sawbench 24, *25*, 28–43, 122, 128
    TGS172 as sawbench 42, *43*, 44, 45
Saw doctor 36, 37
Saw toothed bit 18, *18*
Scale *47*, 48, 49, 59, 68, *74*, 76
Scrap timber 17, *17*, *20*, 32, 33, 52, 68, 69, 89, 91, 95, 128
Screwdriver 131–2, *131*, *132*
Screw feed adjuster 52
Screw knob 52
Set 37, 62, *62*, 63, 71, *72*
Sheet material 10, 38
Shoe 52
Short cuts *58*
Skip tooth 62

Softwood 8, 36, 45, 52, 71, 101, 124, *126*
Soleplate 68, *68*, 69, 87, 89, 90, 93, 128, 129, 130
Spelching 17, 20, 91
Spindle
    of circ. saw 23, 36, 37
    of grinder 115, 116
    of lathe 106, 107, 109, 111
Spindle moulders 10, 11, 91, 93, *93*, 94, *102*, 103, 116, 117, 118–22, *120*, *121*, 135
Splines 33
Splined joint *135*, *136*
Soring 119
Stand 108, 115
Stool 128
Stop block 31, *31*, 32, 48, *59*, 84, 135, 136
Stop rod 83, 84, 85
Sub fence 26, 31, *31*, 32, 33
Sub table
    on bench drill 16, 19
    for mortiser 82, *82*, 83
    for sander *103*
Support 84
    bandsaw 63
    jigsaw 68
    roller 29, *29*, *30*, 31, 32

Table
    of bandsaw 55
    of circ. saw 23, 25, 26
    of disc sander 101
    of mortiser 84, *84*
    of planer/thicknesser 73, *74*, 75, 76, *76*, 77
    of rad. arm 45, *45*, *46*
    of router 93–4
Table insert 25, 31, 57, *58*
Table lamp 108
Table runner 25
Table top 92
Tailstock 107, 108, 109
Take off fence 121
Take off roller 73
Take off table 70, 71, 72
Tankard 108
Taper sawing 34
Teeth 26, 27, *27*, 28, 29, 36, 37, 54, 60, 61, 62, *63*, 69, 126
Telescoping arm 39, 42, *42*
Template *20*, 33, 48, 62, 65
    routing 69, 93, 94, 101, 112, 113, *113*

Tenon 51, *59*, 65, *65*, 86, 135–6, *135*, *137*
Tension 96, 125, 126, 127
Tension adjuster 59, 61, 97, *126*
Thickenessing *see* planer/ thicknesser
Throat 57
Thrust bearing 57, 59, *60*, 61, 65
Tilt
    bandsaw 57, *60*
    bench drill 14
    circ. saw 23, 24, 26, 41, *41*
    fretsaw *126*
    rad. arm 51
Tilt control knot *42*
Tilt scale 48
Tinning 63
Toolrest holder 107, 108, 112
Tooling hazards 9
Topping 37
Torque 131, 132, *132*
Toymakers 69, 130
Track adjuster 59, 60, 61, 97
Trammel arm 69, 92, *92*, 93
Tripod tables 92
Trunnions 57, *60*
Tufnel 93
Turning 52, 65, 92, 105, 108
Tyme
    lathes 111

Universals 70, 117–22, *118*, *119*

V block *17*, 63, 65
Vase 108
Vice 37

Wheels
    two wheeled bandsaws 56, *56*, 57, 59, 60, 61, *61*, 62, 63, 65
    Three wheeled bandsaws 57, *57*
    carborundum wheels 115, *115*
    for toys *103*
Wobble saw 30, 31, 35, 36
Wolf
    electric screwdriver *131*, *132*
    grinder 116, *116*
Wood block *53*
Woodscrew chuck 109
Woodturning *see* Turning
Woodturning tools 106, 110, *110*, 112, 115
Woodworker's square 26, 31, 35
Workmate 41

Yardstick 32